Shuva

YEHUDA KURTZER

# Shuva

The FUTURE of the JEWISH PAST

BRANDEIS UNIVERSITY PRESS

*Waltham, Massachusetts*

Brandeis University Press
An imprint of University Press of New England
www.upne.com

Manufactured in the United States of America
Designed by Kaelin Chappell Broaddus
Typeset in Quadraat OT by Kaelin Chappell Broaddus

University Press of New England is a member of the
Green Press Initiative. The paper used in this book meets
their minimum requirement for recycled paper.

For permission to reproduce any of the material in this book,
contact Permissions, University Press of New England,
One Court Street, Suite 250, Lebanon NH 03766;
or visit www.upne.com

This book was published with the generous support of the
Andrea and Charles Bronfman Philanthropies,
sponsor of the Charles R. Bronfman Visiting Chair in
Jewish Communal Innovation at Brandeis University.

Library of Congress Cataloging-in-Publication Data

Kurtzer, Yehuda.
Shuva: the future of the Jewish past / Yehuda Kurtzer.
p. cm.
Includes bibliographical references and index.

ISBN 978-1-61168-230-4 (cloth: alk. paper)—
ISBN 978-1-61168-231-1 (pbk.: alk. paper)—
ISBN 978-1-61168-232-8 (ebook)

1. Judaism—History—Philosophy.
2. Memory—Religious aspects—Judaism.
3. Commandments (Judaism)
4. Love—Religious aspects—Judaism.
5. Holocaust, Jewish (1939–1945)—Influence.
6. Repentance—Judaism. I. Title.

BM157.K87 2012
296.09—dc23

2011049317

2 3 4 5

Dedicated to my grandparents,
of blessed memory:

JACOB and MINNIE DOPPELT

NATHAN and SYLVIA KURTZER

May their memory always be for a blessing.

There are stars
whose light reaches the earth only after they
      themselves have disintegrated
and are no more.
And there are people
whose scintillating memory lights the world
      after they have passed from it.
These lights—
which shine in the darkest night—are those
      which illumine for us the path.

                        *—Hannah Senesh*

# Contents

# Acknowledgments

This book came about thanks to an extraordinary opportunity created by Charles R. Bronfman and the Andrea and Charles Bronfman Philanthropies, in collaboration with Brandeis University. Mr. Bronfman created a chair at Brandeis for someone to join the faculty for two years and to write a book that "would change the way the Jewish community thinks about itself and its future." It was an absolute honor to serve as the first occupant of the chair, and attempting to meet its expectations was a thrilling challenge.

I am grateful then first and foremost to Charles R. Bronfman, an innovator in Jewish life in the deepest sense of the word, for the willingness to invest in ideas as a key instrument for sustaining the vibrancy of the Jewish people; and to his staff, and specifically Roger Bennett, for respectfully managing this most unusual philanthropic project.

The chair at Brandeis was housed in the Hornstein Program in Jewish Professional Leadership, the foremost graduate program training future Jewish leaders. Jonathan Sarna led the search during his time as chair of the Hornstein Program, and the position was administered subsequently by Len Saxe. Professors Sarna and Saxe are extraordinary mentors and colleagues, and it was a pleasure to have them overseeing my involvement in Hornstein and in the life of the campus, not to mention offering feedback regarding the process and content of this project. Ellen Smith, Rise Singer, and Carol Hengerle are worthy leaders of the Hornstein program and collegial friends, and I am thankful to them for making my experience on campus both seamless and meaningful. The Brandeis students I had the pleasure of teaching—in Hornstein, the Day School Leadership through Teaching program, and the Department of Near Eastern and Judaic Studies—were a terrific and challenging audience with whom to test ideas, and teaching them was always a learning experience for me. Mateo Aceves served as a worthy research assistant, especially with respect to the academic debates on history and memory, and Katie Light helped clean up the manuscript and improved it considerably with her careful eye.

I have taught and lectured widely on pieces of this book in the past few years, and am grateful to the audiences and students for indulging a work in progress, and in many cases for asking incisive questions that improved and refined my arguments. Special thanks go to Jay Moses of the Wexner Foundation and the Heritage groups in Phoenix and Los Angeles; Dov Kahane and the alumni of the Berrie Fellows program in New Jersey; Edgar Bronfman and the staff of the Samuel Bronfman Foundation; Yona Shem-Tov and Bob Chazan and the participants in the Re/Presenting the Jewish Past Conference at New York University; the community at Limmud NY; the board of CAJE in Miami; and Marty Perlmutter and the community at the College of Charleston. Two chapters formed the basis of lectures at Brandeis, and again I am grateful for the intellectual community at the university that so generously welcomed and challenged these ideas. Questions from Ellen Smith, Joe Reimer, and Bill Hamilton especially strengthened the work.

As the reader will discern, the genesis of the ideas in this book precedes my stay at Brandeis, and this is both a personal as well as an academic endeavor. I have benefited from an extraordinary Jewish education but, more important, I have benefited from great and smart friends who have made my learning always personal. I was first challenged to think seriously about commandedness by Josh

Milner and Aliza Sperling Milner, at a Shabbat meal together with Sara Heitler and Kenny Bamberger. Such conversations ultimately coincided with a research fellowship at the United States Holocaust Memorial Museum in 2004, and since then I have been working through the relationship between commandedness and the memory of the recent past. I am grateful to Paul Shapiro and Ann Millin for allowing me to explore the intersection of Jewish studies and Holocaust studies at the Center for Advanced Holocaust Studies, even as my research and findings seemed culturally—and at times conceptually—at odds with others' research at the Center. I am always indebted to the Wexner Foundation for inspiring in me a belief in the unity of passionate Jewish leadership and serious Jewish thinking. I completed the book while beginning a new position with The Shalom Hartman Institute, an organization I am proud to help lead. The institute is bringing serious conversation on major issues to Jewish leaders and change-agents, and modeling both thought-leadership and sophisticated discourse for the betterment of Jewish life. This book was considerably improved by my joining the intellectual community at SHI, and through my exposure to the people and ideas that define the institution. In particular, I am grateful to work with and learn from my friend, boss, and teacher, Rabbi Donniel Hartman; and I am deeply grateful to my friends and colleagues Suzanne Kling and Rabbi Lauren Berkun for reading portions of the manuscript and—together with the rest of our terrific team—for doing the work of bringing some of these ideas into practice.

Many friends and teachers have helped this intellectual journey along its way, whether as constant dialogue partners or as onetime coffee dates, indulging my many questions. These friends include: Marc Baker, Aviva Bock, Jacob Cytryn, Jon Levisohn, Ami Butler, Jessica Radin, David Shatz, Ethan Tucker, Elie Kaunfer, Josh Foer, Jay Pomrenze, David Wolpe, David Myers, J. J. Schachter, Rae Janvey, and many more. Professor Shaye Cohen taught me how to be a historian, and I am grateful for his mentorship. I learned a great deal from the members of the Shalom Hartman Institute's North American Scholars Circle, and on the issues in this book especially from a talk by Laura Levitt. Most recently I have benefited from the ongoing learning I am privileged to do with Sharon Cohen Anisfeld, Jack Wertheimer, Steven M. Cohen, and Suzanne Last Stone. Danya Ruttenberg helped me through a tough stretch, and I return to her insightful advice often. Yael Bendat-Appell read portions of the manuscript; I am grateful for her many wise comments and for an enduring friendship.

The manuscript was also aided considerably by the comments from the two readers solicited by the publisher and dramatically improved with the careful and generous editing of the copy editor, Jason Warshof. Sylvia Fuks Fried, Phyllis Deutsch, and the great people at Brandeis University Press have been gracious partners in shepherding this project and have improved the book in innumerable ways. Mindy Weisel was so kind to lend her stunning painting All That Is Remembered to serve as a fitting cover to this work, and as a marker of her friendship.

My family is a constant source of support: My parents, Dan and Sheila Kurtzer, attend my lectures, read my work, and offer both meaningful feedback and the underrated but equally important parental affirmation. My in-laws, Ed and Dolly Ives, hung in with a son-in-law who mostly wanted to spend his time thinking, saying all along that perhaps someday a book might come of it. My brothers, David and Jacob, frame my understanding of my own upbringing and challenge me constantly with their differing interpretations of the same data; my sons, Noah and Jesse, provide the context essential for everything I write about continuity. Most of all, Stephanie Ives, my wife and partner in every sense of the word, helps me create the home that fulfills and enables our aspirations, and helps me imagine the bridge between big ideas and the life we hope they inform.

This book is about memory and the passage of time. I am saddened that my grandparents are not alive to see the publication of this book, which feels so much like a statement of a Jewishness that I inherited from them and strive to transmit to my children. It is my hope that my memories of them—the ones I own, and the ones that I continue to form—will withstand the passage of time and continue to be commanding in my life. This book is dedicated to my grandparents' memory.

*Shuva*

# From Memory to History

The opposite of the past is not the future but the
absence of future; the opposite of the future is not
the past but the absence of past. The loss of one is
equivalent to the sacrifice of the other.
—Elie Wiesel, "Hope, Despair, and Memory"
(Nobel Lecture), December 11, 1986

Once upon a time, the past was present, and the future was redemptive and hopeful. Never mind that the present was itself forgettable;
the premodern world was probably not fun to inhabit, especially for
Jews. Still, this arc of time and the way Jews related to it were useful.
The past provided context and purpose, the future lent hope and optimism, and the present—well, the present was often awful, but in
the words of one of the great sages in Mishnah Avot, the world was
anyway just a hallway—a *prozdor*—through which we pass to the
banquet hall of whatever comes next.

To be sure, as Rabbi Jacob goes on to say in that same passage, one moment of repentance and good deeds in this world exceeds all there is to find on the other side. There is meaning in how one walks through the hallway; even in its darkest times, classical Judaism never became so nihilistic, or obsessed with the "next world," at the cost of participating actively in this one. Jewish leaders have generally succeeded at articulating a sense of mission in spite of, and still directed toward, ultimate salvation on the other side. Nevertheless, the premodern Jewish experience held together in part because of this view of time, because of the unique ability to bind the stuff of the past with the stuff of destiny. This system—drawing fodder from the past, which drove action in the present toward a purposeful future—was strong enough to *absorb* calamity rather than be destroyed or consumed by it. This consciousness of the past, the ability to take a "usable" past and strengthen the present, became a forceful marker of identity.

Since the modern turn—with all of its enlightening and emancipating, its unfettering of chains ideological, political, and collective—Jews have tended to leave the mythic imagination behind. One of the great ironies of modern Jewish life is that we now know much more about our origins, our history, and our ancestry than we ever did before; and as a collective, we care about it considerably less. The key system by which Jews relate to their past has changed to "history"—in many ways the corollary or sometimes the antithesis of memory. History has served as the hallmark of the powerful critiques of Jewishness characterizing the modern period, those from both within and without. The reformers of Judaism in the eighteenth and nineteenth centuries fixated on the study of Jewish history, particularly in the ancient world, as a means of uncovering the "true origins" of the faith, usually with the intent of stripping away the accumulated dust of medievality and rabbinism to get to what was essential. Scholars and critics have used historical methods to deconstruct Jewish myths of origin, nationality, oppression, and uniqueness in seeking either the triumph of their own breed of particularism or in championing some denuded universalism. As early as Spinoza on the authorship of the Bible, as recently as today, with political agendas ranging from the validation of Jewish sovereignty over Biblical Israel to the questioning of the conventional narrative of the Holocaust, the principal tool in Jewish argumentation is historical. Validity lies in empirical demonstration; to borrow Jacob Neusner's felicitous phrase, "What we cannot show, we do not know."

Memory, in contrast, with its architecture of mythology, its obligations and recitations, and its reliance on the raw vulnerability of the human mind, stands little chance of surviving in this climate of the empirical and the rational. Both of these modes, history and memory, entail looking backward in time toward achieving progress, but memory seems hopelessly quaint and downright ineffective in comparison with history's brute force. Still, the contemporary surfeit of Jewish museums, archaeology, and scholarship has not suppressed or resolved an anxiety about our growing distance from our past as much as they have caused it to surface. The loss of the past is a source of confusion, anxiety, and concern in Jewish life. Among the aspects of modernity that create anxiety about present and future, the loss of memory—with its unique meanings to Jewish consciousness, and its creative force in Jewish thought—feels catastrophic. Memory has worked for Jews before; can it be rehabilitated?

This book argues for a kind of collective transformation of Jewish life through the selective reclamation of the past, and a translation of that past into purposefulness. This process may be called "memory," and this act or process represents not just a classical technique of Jewish survival but perhaps the very key to Jewish cultural thriving. The modern Jewish experience has by and large rejected this mode of thinking and is therefore less good at remembering, a decision and a failure that have not served us well, and I want to argue that memory both can and should be reclaimed. Memory can become paradoxically both a vehicle of progress and dependent on the stuff of old; and a consciousness driven by cognizance of our origins may be the best hope for thinking about where we are headed. In this book, I propose a system of thought and a reading strategy for our texts and our past, in order to articulate a Jewishness that stands in radical relationship to the past without attempting to inhabit it.

---

To better understand the mandate of this book, let us expand and define the problem. I want to consider four discrete examples, what I would call "conceptual moments," that reflect the contemporary Jewish experience and the growing estrangement from our past—and the growing consciousness of the costs associated with this estrangement:

First of all, there is a profound disconnect between what Jewish memory once meant and how memory is deployed today. Perhaps the best example lies in the liturgical calendar. The Jewish calendar features a long and heavily ritualized "memory season," which starts in earnest on Shabbat Zakhor, the Shabbat of "Remember!" immediately preceding Purim. Exactly one month later comes Passover and its reenactments, fulfilling our obligation to see ourselves living through a key moment in the Jewish past. Between Passover and Shavuot we mark a kind of extended mourning period to remember the slain students of Rabbi Akiva, a stretch that in the more recent past has been punctuated with Yom HaShoah, Holocaust Remembrance Day, and Yom HaZikaron, Israel's memorial day for its fallen soldiers. After Shavuot, which marks the anniversary of the giving of the Torah, memory season wanes. But it picks up again later in the summer with the fast days commemorating the great catastrophes and destructions of the Jewish past. The Ninth of Av is the most famous and pronounced, accumulating darkness and attracting historical catastrophes like a magnet. Of course, a key to survival is the assignment of a place to collect the darkness; without the Ninth of Av, we would either spend the year in mourning or would desperately strive to forget all the accumulated catastrophes. Still, the Ninth of Av is like the anti-Passover—with all suffering and no liberation—and the two days together are the archetypical days of memory on the Jewish calendar.

And yet, for all the consistency in this framework, the memory season is actually deeply fragmented: the rituals within it are inconsistent, the various memories they evoke are dissimilar, and the meaning of memory altogether seems to vary. On Shabbat Zakhor we fulfill the biblical mandate to remember the treachery of the people of Amalek by publicly reciting aloud from the Torah the very obligation to remember; we do not so much remember the event *itself* as the obligations that emerge from its memory. How then do we remember Amalek? We remember Amalek by recommitting ourselves to the biblical prohibition against forgetting Amalek; or more specifically, by recommitting ourselves to the somewhat paradoxical command to not forget to eliminate the memory. The fulfillment of this command, or at least its translation into a relevant mythical example, comes several days later with the reading of the Purim story. This story depicts the villainous Haman as the direct descendant of Amalek, thus bringing to life the ongoing responsibility that we remember Amalek's treachery as fundamentally relevant to our own lives and endeavor to stamp out its memory. The Purim story, as it bridges a biblical commandment with a second manifestation said to take place hundreds of years later, invites the listeners to "pay it forward," to vigilantly stay aware of existential and genocidal threats, and to celebrate our triumph over them. It has not been difficult for Jews to translate Purim even further into contemporary relevance; Purim has become a template on which one may create a celebratory holiday to mark having emerged unscathed from a dangerous situation. The legendary shriek of convicted Nazi Julius Streicher on the moment of his execution—"Purimfest 1946!" confirms the means by which a legendary and mythical account serves as an anchor in our memory through which we route and understand significant events in our collective imagination.

Passover and Shavuot also ritualize the past as their acts of memory. Passover picks up this thread of existential menace introduced on Purim as part of its liturgy—we are meant to sing, in a melody that at least in my household was dissonantly upbeat given the horrifying message, that in "every generation, there are those who would rise up to destroy us; but the Holy Blessed One saves us from their hands." This is the memory, even if the reality has been less salvific. In any case, when we recount the Exodus on the Passover night, we mostly tell stories about how people have told stories about the Exodus, as a kind of modeling exercise on how we might tell stories in our living rooms. We learn to get so swept up in the ongoing relevance of the messages of liberation and deliverance that we would not notice that morning had already come. Passover does not feature survivor testimonials; it features the fantasies and the musings of the descendants of those survivors, who know very well that memory becomes more magical, fantastical, and commanding in the hands of those who are less bound by what actually transpired and more inspired by what they might learn from it. So too on Shavuot night—since the days of the Kabbalists in the sixteenth century, Jews have attempted to repair (l'taken) the failure of the Israelites to properly prepare for the giving of the Torah by staying awake all night, as though we might retroactively correct this historical mistake and enter the covenant anew—and this time on better terms.

But the modern holidays—Yom HaShoah and Yom HaZikaron —do not look anything like these templates. These two commemoration days, invented in recent generations and inserted into the liturgical calendar, stand out as entirely phenomenologically different. Perhaps this is deliberate, in that the architects of these days did not want them subsumed within the liturgical calendar and within religious frameworks. This foreignness also stems from a host of political considerations that defined the founding of the holidays, as J. J. Schachter writes, and that created internecine Jewish conflict around their invention. But it leaves us modern inheritors in something of a lurch. On Passover, we insert ourselves into a narrative, we become the oppressed and the liberated; on Yom HaShoah, the custom has emerged that we become passive listeners to a survivor, to an eyewitness. On Passover, we toy with a template and make it relevant; on Yom HaShoah, our memory is dictated by listening to the precise recitation of specific events. The calendar almost becomes a metaphor itself for the disjuncture of modernity—these new days thematically resonate with their calendrical forbears, even as they differ significantly.

Memory, the act of remembering, comes to mean two completely different and even opposing things. The remembering that characterizes Purim and Passover is malleable and playful: we remember Amalek by playing out its treachery at other times in Jewish history and even our own; we remember the Exodus by trying to relive it—not by traveling through time but by privileging the centrality of its message of liberation in our own time. But the commanding memory of the Holocaust in our present climate, in and out of

Yom HaShoah, is precisely the opposite—it is a memory that fears forgetting, a memory for which the passing of time and the loss of precision seem ominous and fearful, a memory that has generated the cataloging of testimonials and the furious documentation of experiences lest the eyewitnesses themselves depart and take with them our memories. Is this really memory?

Second: almost three decades ago the eminent Jewish historian Yosef Hayim Yerushalmi set the stage for this discussion, and for the divide between history and memory as opposing orientations. In his little book *Zakhor*, Yerushalmi threaded together his own reflections on the Jewish past with the growing field of memory studies, and made a novel argument: whereas Jews had once related to their past through techniques of memory, the disjuncture of the Enlightenment had brought about a turn to history instead. Jews were always interested in their past, but not in chronicling the past meticulously, as historiography demands. Rather, they channeled it to Jewish life quite differently. Memory is selective, deliberate, literary, constructed, and oriented toward the lessons we take from the past; history, in this binary, is scientific and empirical. Memory, played out in ritual and recital, is an act of embracing the past; history, of understanding the past—even if that understanding can create a deep alienation between the past and the present. Yerushalmi went on to declare Jewish memory all but dead, superseded by a different and in some ways unprecedented interest in Jewish history.

In Yerushalmi's eloquent formulation, this turn from memory to history was permanent and irreversible, and left modern Jews in need of new bridge-builders to the past. Yerushalmi did not disavow the importance of the Jewish past to a vibrant Jewish present; but he no longer saw the mechanisms of memory capable of holding the hearts of enlightened and emancipated Jews. Yerushalmi hoped that this role of building a bridge to the Jewish past would fall to Jewish historians themselves. If historians are responsible for the demythologization of the Jewish past, perhaps they then become responsible for managing the new relationship to the Jewish past that emerges. If you break it, you own it.

Having constructed this history-memory binary on the basis of collective memory studies, Yerushalmi declared history the winner and the historians the reluctant champions, placing a heavy mantle of responsibility on himself and his fellow craftsmen. Yerushalmi perhaps hoped that some building blocks to identity would remain in the work of the historian, that a scientific understanding of the Jewish past could still be marshaled in the right hands for constructive ends. This would prove challenging both for those historians who cherished the role of bridge-builder to the past—those for whom a desire to connect past with present motivated their entry into the study of history—and especially those for whom history constituted a secular and liberating pastime from the burdensome mantle of the past. Even for those who would succeed at such an endeavor, the path is treacherous: to take a scientific approach to the past and make it constructive of identity, and not subject to the basic critique to which memory had become vulnerable, is tricky work indeed. History acknowledges the place of memory as a foregoing stage on an evolutionary path. The premise of evolution is that what comes before is fundamentally inferior, or at least insufficiently adaptive. The instinct of those who would use the tools of history for the betterment of culture or identity often relies on the assumption that we are correcting for the mistakes of the past, learning its lessons—without seeking to actually dwell in it.

Now, since the book appeared, Yerushalmi has been critiqued as much as he has been feted. The book both serves as a central feature of Jewish history curricula, and as the subject of extensive scholarly debate and disagreement. Driven first and foremost by Amos Funkenstein, Yerushalmi's critics and students disputed, finessed, and attenuated his claims: Jews were not willfully ignorant or dismissive of history even if their means of expressing it or articulating it were not conventionally historiographical. Others focused on the polarization that necessarily stemmed from Yerushalmi using such a rigid heuristic, so drastically charting a difference between history and memory. Scholars have argued that there are intermediate categories between these poles, and ways in which history has perpetuated memory or memory literature has served, with all its complexity, in the writing of history. And still others have endeavored to show that the predictions and laments at the end of *Zakhor* have not been fulfilled—that either the historians fall short of what

Yerushalmi hoped or that the work of memory seems to persist in spite of Yerushalmi's despairing claim of its disappearance.

The attention paid to Yerushalmi is itself a form of data; it reflects the sense in which Yerushalmi identified the spark of a problem, and rather majestically named this tension around memory as a direct product of the Jewish encounter with the modern world. This question of relevance and empowerment remains a vibrant one for the academy and for scholars of Jewish studies; I would say (albeit anecdotally) that the whole generation of Jewish historians that has emerged since Zakhor, including myself, is informed by its message and troubled by its mandate. We are left to wonder: is knowledge of the past a moral responsibility? Does knowledge of the past necessarily make us superior to it? In my own study and then teaching of Jewish history, I perpetually ask myself: if I went in search of the Jewish past in order to say something meaningful to the Jewish present and future, which language—that of the historian or that of the memorialist—would have a more lasting resonance? And frankly, is this really the work of the historian, searching the past in order to find the present?

That history should ineffectively tell our story is not a problem confined to the American Jewish community. Contemporary Jews who live in Israel also suffer from a memory problem, although theirs is of a different nature. Collective memory in Israel is fraught and heavily politicized, and the ramifications of how and what the society remembers have implications for public policy on a more obvious and immediate level. On one hand, the Israeli literary tradition as embodied in its giants—Dan Pagis, Aharon Appelfeld, even Yehuda Amichai—conveys a deep heaviness about Israeli society as weighted and burdened by the Holocaust. The past matters to these titans of Israeli letters—or, even more starkly, the past is unavoidable in precisely the commanding way in which memory works. Appelfeld, for instance, is famous for noting that there is no end to Holocaust narrative; the lesser-known but equally significant Pagis renders the survivor experience into biblical myth and language, and in doing so sears the real and mythic Jewish past into the formative development of the Hebrew language and Israeli consciousness. On the other hand, the state of Israel is no longer predominantly

Ashkenazi and now lacks common defining historical experiences for the majority of its citizenry beyond the experiences within the state proper.

Meantime, much of the last generation of historical scholarship in the public arena in Israel has revolved around the "new historians," the revisionists who questioned and then meticulously undermined the mythical narratives of Israel's origins and history. From reframing Israel as the superior power in 1948 rather than an underdog, to rendering more complex the morass created by the British with their conflicting promises, to portraying the dark and shadowy relationship between the rise of the state and the unfolding of the Holocaust in Europe, the legacy of this era in historical scholarship gave a jolt to memory in as dramatic fashion as Jews have experienced in modernity.

At the same time, Israel's younger Jews—and many diaspora Jews who have experienced Israel only in the past few generations—have rarely grown up themselves on the mythology of miracles as much as the memory of trauma. The assassination of Yitzhak Rabin is the most likely analogy for younger Jews to the 1967 elation of a previous generation, and the rise of the state to the one before that. The past sixteen years since the assassination have seen countless terror attacks, several difficult and controversial battles and wars, a country severed by political extremism, and an increasing alienation in the world community. For some, this is the formative stuff of memory that makes for stronger identity; certainly Jewish history has precedent in turning victimhood—real or imagined—into self-definition. For others, meanwhile, the absence of a core mythic narrative, shattered by revisionism, and an ongoing positive mythic experience, is devastating to the future of Israel's mythic identity.

In one particularly public case, one of the new historians attempted to do what Yerushalmi prescribed—to pick up the identity pieces that he had shattered and reinstate something out of them. Benny Morris's study of the 1948 war and the ensuing refugee problem was the cause célèbre of the entire new revisionist history paradigm, with its exhaustive and detailed analysis of Israeli direct expulsions of Palestinians and attendant atrocities. Although celebrated by the left, part of Morris's appeal to historians and empiricists was his diffidence toward politics. Some of Morris's colleagues did their work via journalistic outlets and publishing houses, but less because of a leaning toward the work of investigation and advocacy and more out of practical necessity: the universities would not hire them. So, for Morris, the project was ostensibly about history and not identity. Morris made these sentiments clear, echoing the culture of the historian we saw earlier in the discussion of Yerushalmi: Morris saw himself as merely a reader of the evidence, evidence that required eyes more than an interpretation. History, in a certain sense, was on his side; the new historians were among the first to excavate previously sealed archival records. Morris and his "revisionist" colleagues were not political operatives, in this portrayal; they were merely documenting the facts, even as those facts served an implicit yet obvious political agenda.

Perhaps out of guilt, perhaps out of a change of heart, perhaps because we are to take Morris at his word that his scholarship was *always* genuinely dispassionate and separate from political realities, and perhaps because Morris believed Yerushalmi that his debunking now gave him ownership over Israeli-Jewish identity, Morris made some astonishing political pronouncements a few years ago, to the tune of acknowledging Israel's history of atrocities and suggesting that perhaps they had not gone far enough. A far cry from documenting the atrocities alone, which served to question the legitimacy of the ultranationalist camp, Morris now joined that very camp. Although Morris's colleagues were surprised by this pronouncement, and although it confirmed a larger shift in Israeli attitudes away from optimism and toward a sad kind of realpolitik approach to their chronic political crisis, the reaction to Morris was not parallel to that of his previous work. Morris's political views were startling, but not groundbreaking. The force of shattering Israeli mythology *the first time around* was much stronger, given the credence lent to its effort by facts and figures, by the tools of empiricism. At the end of the process, Morris was merely another disaffected leftist—broken by history, equally broken by what history had left behind.

Now Morris is not the average Israeli, and the politics of memory play out very differently across the political spectrum. But the

Morris case hints at the way in which memory anxiety is playing out in how Israel relates its understanding of its past to its present and future. The Israeli Jewish community too has seen a renaissance of Jewish learning, of a craving for the vehicles and language of a Jewish past to help yield a sense of authentic belonging in the choices of the present. In Israel too, however, a failure to place this craving in an ideological context, a failure to understand what it is we sense that we have lost, may produce short-term and even misguided attempts to grasp at programmatic solutions to a more sophisticated problem. Israeli society was at its core built on a hybridization of past paradigms with modern ideas. Some of those modern ideas have been debunked or jettisoned, and some of those past paradigms have shown themselves to be insufficient. And American Jewish affiliation with Israel was premised on living through miraculous events and holding on to non-transmissible personal memories. Can Zionism—for Israeli society, and for American Jews—rehabilitate the memory that it once so effectively marshaled?

Third: memory and the proper use of the past, it seems, are a pivotal hinge in defining the core questions of Jewish affiliational life. In 1999, the Reform movement revisited the epochal "Pittsburgh Platform" of a century earlier, which had radically reenvisioned Judaism and Jewish national identity for the features of modernity in 1885. Now the movement restated as the essential elements of Reform Judaism the basic tenets of God, Torah, and Israel. Laid alongside the original Pittsburgh Platform—with its fierce declamation of "Mosaic and rabbinical laws" as foreign to modern milieus—the new document articulated a vision for progressive Judaism that sounds downright reactionary, an ironic turn for a progressive movement. The celebration of modernity as evolutionarily superior, which characterized the 1885 credo, disappeared now in favor of a more subversive—and perhaps more effective—hybrid of the modern scene with the wineskins of tradition and a sacred past.

Then in 2001, in a Conservative synagogue in Los Angeles, Rabbi David Wolpe delivered a sermon on Passover in which he first outlined the historical and archaeological evidence that militates against the Bible's telling of the Exodus story. He then challenged his congregation with the difficult and provocative charge that they are *nevertheless* obligated to remember the day they left Egypt, per the biblical commandment to that effect, for the rest of their lives. Wolpe's speech—or, perhaps more accurately, the timing and assumptions that motivated the speech—was roundly criticized, for reasons ranging from his assumption that a Conservative Jewish audience already disbelieved the Torah's telling of events (which turned out to not be true) to the more far-fetched but politically relevant association of Wolpe's discrediting of the Exodus with the effort to erase Israel's archaeological record and historical narrative toward a pro-Palestinian political outcome.

Needless to say, few accounts dealt effectively with the second half of Wolpe's speech, which was by far more sophisticated and inspiring than the deflating first half. Sophisticated Jewish thought is less newsworthy than controversy. Wolpe was articulating a profound posthistorical, postmodern theology for Jewishness, commitment, and obligation, a theology that in part inspires this book. He argued convincingly that we are bound to the narrative of the Exodus and its aftermath *even if* it is only a story, and even if our historical tools make it an unlikely story at that. Now, this turn is not *entirely* posthistorical. In his book *Resisting History*, the historian David Myers notes the irony in Wolpe's use of critical historical tools in deconstructing the Exodus, that ultimately Wolpe does not and cannot reject these tools because they have become so essential to who we are. In essence, historical tools are part of what we use to sever our ties from history itself. Wolpe's speech signals a pivotal move in a denomination defined by its association with the positive-historical orientation toward a sensibility that begins to divorce the full implications of the historical from the covenantal core that it is helping to elucidate.

In the meantime, in 1995 Haim Soloveitchik—a chronicler of Jewish history and through his family lineage a participant therein—published a deeply personal yet scholarly invective about the culture increasingly permeating contemporary Orthodoxy, a move from the mimetic to the book-learning in shaping Orthodox religious life and practice. In his celebrated essay "Rupture and Reconstruction," Soloveitchik echoed Yerushalmi in identifying moments in modernity that shattered previously held paradigms, though for Soloveitchik the epochal moment—the "rupture" in the title—was not the Enlightenment but rather the Holocaust. But in showing the ways in which popular piety was shifting, in how Jewish law learned from a book makes for a radicalized culture unknown to perfectly pious ancestors, Soloveitchik exposed how Orthodoxy too suffered from a memory problem: Orthodoxy was equally "unrooted." While still tethered to what ostensibly seem like past paradigms—traditional behaviors and mores, religious practice, in some cases a premodern sensibility about knowledge and enlightenment—these claims and ideologies rested not on a continuous narrative chain with the past, Soloveitchik demonstrated, but on an altogether new and artificially constructed bridge. Soloveitchik saw these moves, which entail the ceding of much greater power to rabbinic authority, and which continue to produce a high aesthetic sensibility within evolving Orthodoxy, as reflecting a fundamental lack of confidence in authenticity among Orthodox Jews, and a resulting lack of access to authority and power. The consequence was that the learned few elites were accumulating much more authority than they had held in previous generations. In essence, Orthodoxy too was becoming something entirely new and disconnected from its mythic origins.

These stories are not the same and only vaguely parallel one another. Soloveitchik and Wolpe are less prescriptive than is the new Pittsburgh Platform, and each story has its idiosyncrasies that resist being grouped with the others. But taken together, these three "moments" triangulate a problem, and suggest a shift in Jewish life: we now recognize that this basic loss of memory, this inability to connect naturally and organically with the flow of a past into the present, has yielded difficult implications for lived Jewishness in any of these ideological systems. The loss of a mythic past affects and implicates all of us. Soloveitchik names a problem, Wolpe theorizes about what it looks like on the other side, and the Reform movement grasps at the pieces that it sees as authentic remnants of the past, those that might survive into the present and future. This is all the stuff of anxiety in search of an organizing principle.

And fourth, the most familiar site of anxiety about memory and its loss lies in the constant reminders that we hear in our families and institutions about the imminent demise of the generations that survived the Holocaust, in the burgeoning of an American Jewish community increasingly populated both by converts and nonconverts whose instinctive cultural memory is quite different, in the precarious ways in which the Jewish community tries to create affiliation with Israel predicated on historical realities not experienced by Jews born after 1967, and in the incessant construction of museums of Jewish life and culture that, in the darker moments, feels like anxious preservation in the face of a growing sense of loss. We have now recorded countless hours of oral testimonies on film: does this not feel like an anxious response, the work of fear and concern?

These are four very different examples, but I see them stemming from a systemic problem. My approach here is to find language and a framework with which to confront it. As Tony Judt writes:

> . . . of all our contemporary illusions, the most dangerous is the one that underpins and accounts for all the others. And that is the idea that we live in a time without precedent: that what is happening to us is new and irreversible and that the past has nothing to teach us . . . except when it comes to ransacking it for serviceable precedents.

I want to make the case here that—to extrapolate from Yerushalmi—the distinction between history and memory does not merely describe how we talk or write about the past, but characterizes in a much deeper way who we actually are, that memory is an essential feature of Jewishness. *We are a people of memory.* The transitions suggested by the modern experience, then, have not merely brought the acquisition of new tools by which to think about the past, but possibly a seismic shift in who we have become; perhaps if we change how we think about our past, we change who we are.

To make this work, we must convincingly make the case for an orientation toward the past that does not whitewash its failures and inadequacies. Much as I have stated here that the loss of memory has been catastrophic, I am also concerned about how awareness of memory gets reasserted. As a historian, I fear that too dramatic a swing will entail an attempt to reject history and its tools altogether.

Not everything old is good, and very little of the experience of life in the past would qualify as better than the lives we live now; history, applied correctly, is an ethical tool by which we use our consciousness of what has preceded us to make better and more informed choices for the future. I think we need to be concerned by the anti- or posthistorical move when it necessarily vilifies the gifts of historiography, or demands of us an antirational stance that we should not be obliged to take. Somehow we want to be people of history and people of memory.

We also do not want to overmythologize the past, as though Tevye the Dairyman represented the high point of Jewish history and ideals. The tendency toward this nostalgic mythmaking does not just risk our choosing the wrong archetypes, it also risks forcing the complexity of Jewish ethnicity and diversity into a single and dominant narrative. A systemic approach to Jewish memory must tolerate a multiplicity of fore-narratives, such that both secularism and religiosity can be anchored as Jewish choices with historical continuity, as well as all the permutations in between. It must also figure out a way to make major episodes of Jewish history feature in the consciousness of people who are not the direct descendants of their protagonists. There must be a system through which the Holocaust becomes culturally defining for Middle Eastern Jews, and through which the memory of a midnight flight from Tunis features into the collective memory of Ashkenazim. At the same time, this system cannot reduce these experiences in such a way that mocks the personal complexity of individual experience.

Moreover, in the sea of programs and institutions that have arisen to take ownership of the Jewish past, we must recognize that many of these enlist the language of memory in the ironic service of history. Oftentimes the attempts to hold on to past "stuff" become obsessively historical, choosing not to sift for what needs to be kept and what can go into long-term storage. This hearkens back to Yerushalmi and his lament that the profession of history inclines us toward a veneration of the arcane, and toward the weird ideology of believing that everything from the past has its own story and deserves to be preserved. When the process of trying to retain the stuff of the past fails to develop systems of evaluation—when it preserves a whole library without creating an exhibition case—we wind up equally unaided in our attempts to actually make and transmit meaning of everything we now have. An unused library, even if impressive, gets dusty; and this attempt to revalue the Jewish past must come together with a language that articulates value and systems by which it gets used. And this, knowing all the while that in that very use the stuff will change and will even mean something different to us than it "originally" meant.

No, memory has to be an elastic and selective system that still operates with intellectual honesty and integrity, a system that makes the past serviceable in search of a redemptive future. The system has to be both plausible with respect to the past that it is hoping to use and malleable to the modern realities and ethics that govern our lives. What's more, we have to consider the role of collective consciousness, and what it will look like to recreate the productive instability of inhabiting both past and present. The theory of cognitive dissonance, as proposed by Leon Festinger, asserts that it is difficult to hold two conflicting ideas in our mind simultaneously, that this dissonance results in a deep psychological discomfort. The classic examples that Festinger discusses in his work hinge on the experience of "disconfirmed expectancy"—such as a failed prophecy, or the moment in which an individual or group realizes that its expectation has not and will not come to pass. Such instances include the early Christians' response to Christ's crucifixion and subsequent nonreturn and, as has been documented using Festinger's research, Lubavitch Jews' response to the death of their beloved Rebbe after some of his followers had crowned him the messiah incarnate.

According to this theory, which has held tremendous currency in both medical and psychological research, the dissonance produced by this disconfirmation is uncomfortable, and inclines the individual or the group to actively resolve that dissonance. This can be accomplished by disconfirming one of the two issues, realities, or experiences that are producing the tension. What was so astonishing about Festinger's discovery was that the obvious issue does not get discredited or disconfirmed: so the death of a charismatic leader who appeared to be superhuman does not automatically obliterate the previously held belief that the person was in fact immortal or superhuman. To discredit that view would be, in many cases, more traumatic than rejecting the much more plausible reality that the person was in fact dead. And so the route out of dissonance often travels through implausibility in search of stability.

Here, cognitive dissonance may be a useful metaphor to think about this history-memory divide or, even more ambitiously, as a metaphor to think about the broader challenge evinced by the modern Jewish experience, between myth and empiricism. Dissonance is a key feature of the contemporary Jewish lived experience; it feels difficult to sustain an attentiveness to texts and traditions that derive from a fundamentally, systemically particularistic worldview while gazing at the attractive universalism around us. Wolpe gave voice to the conflict between empirical knowledge and spiritually perceived truth, and we find conflict as well in the legitimacy of parallel truths—be they conflicting Jewish ideas or historical narratives. We have the paradigm of the sovereign self as marker of the modern Jewish character, and of the commanded self that characterizes much of our paradigmatic literature and ethics. How are these supposed to live side by side, much less inhabit the same hearts and minds? At the risk of being overly programmatic: does our Judaism require that we shut off parts of our brain when we live, alternatively, in synagogue or street?

Our central question involves how we resolve that dissonance and emerge stable on the other side. The easy answers tend to involve the rejection of one of the poles, either in the fundamentalist retreat from universalism and empiricism or the liberal drift from particularism and local tradition. Even these are far from absolute, and I would suggest that invariably not only do most Jews fall confusingly between these two choices, but even that any choice is specific only to the individuals of one generation. Assimilation, accommodation, acculturation—the basic techniques through which Jews inhabit the spheres of particularism and universalism simultaneously and navigate the conflict between them—are actually moving targets, the categories evolving all the time relative to new generations of Jews and new iterations of old problems.

But there are two other models in responding to dissonance that require our thinking and consideration and that do not involve the reductive—and I think ultimately failed—approach of shutting down or rejecting conflicting truths that are actually truths. If you do not actually believe in one or the other, or if you do not believe that the truths characterize Jewishness or modern life, the conflict is significantly attenuated; the problem is only sharp when the two truths are held together, at the same time, and exist in conflict with one another. What would it look like to ask if—discomfort notwithstanding—we can endeavor to actually exist in that dissonance? Or further, what would it look like not just to inhabit the dissonance but to think about harmonizing these dissonant ideas—not rejecting one or the other in the quest for total clarity but trying to find ways to speak in a language that incorporates both as necessary qualifiers and filters of each other? If we talk about the sovereign self and the commanded self, must we stake the claim that commandedness and self-sovereignty are opposite? Is there a way to understand both commandedness and sovereignty in ways that make them complementary? If we talk about empiricism and master-myth, are we required to jettison one or the other—or can we find language that enables us to live with both? And again, this may still result in a dissonance. Can we tolerate that dissonance? Is that dissonance perhaps a small price to pay for a complex identity?

Rabbi Yitz Greenberg provides one model with which to deal with a post-Holocaust reality that upsets the paradigm of "true convictions." Greenberg suggests that the key lesson from the Nazi ideology that yielded mass death by demanding monolithic orthodoxy is the realization that truth only exists in a broken state, that every truth claim exists somewhere on the scale of truth but is not absolutely verifiable. In echoing the theologian Eliezer Berkovits's claim for the mutual legitimacy of both the survivor who walked out of the camps having lost faith and those who interpreted their experience to increase their faith, Greenberg's paradigm argues for a belief in the pluralism of partial truths. It is not so much that we are faced with multiple truths, each of which bears 100 percent accuracy, and struggle to accommodate them with each other; we actually bear no full truths, and so we must acknowledge, respect, and even to some degree incorporate truths that we do not fully believe into our understanding of who we are. Greenberg's model reduces our experience of dissonance by contesting the notion that each idea or value should hold absolute sway. The result then is that this lesser dissonance is something we can live with. Truths pass each other in the night in our minds and our lives, and the sense of conflict is dampened. The risk inherent in Greenberg's paradigm, which he does not acknowledge, is the descent to nihilism: the sense that since we cannot speak of absolute truths, we must be skeptical or dismissive of ideas and convictions that require obedience, subservience, or belief.

The question remains, though, whether other routes may lead us out of this dissonance—or whether other means may exist to inhabit it—and toward a holistic and optimistic lived Jewish modernity. One of my tasks here is to understand the dissenting aspects of contemporary Jewish experience in such a way that they become not just compatible but a useful paradigm. I believe that the essential elements of Jewish tradition and the Jewish past—whether we classify them as Torah, Service, and Lovingkindness, or Prayer, Study, and Reflection—and which I take together as the work of memory—served once, and may continue to serve, as a strategy for adaptation. In some ways the present, with all its nuances and complexities, is the most historically compatible epoch to the time in which classical Jewish civilization was born. A cognizance of this compatibility enables us to read the past as much more relevant and contemporary than it appears.

And finally, our definition of memory must also take into account the developments in brain research that speak to the processes of memory and how the mind stores information. The neurobiologist Eric Kandel has spent a lifetime in Nobel Prize–winning research, achieving an unprecedented integration of brain science with psychology in his search for memory, building a discipline that he describes as "a new science of the mind." Kandel demonstrated how chemical activity in synapses produces long-term memory storage. This, in turn, generates what he provocatively calls "learning." Kandel calls memory "the glue that binds the mental life together" and the vehicle that "allows us to get continuity in our lives." Kandel's work—narrated magnificently in his book *In Search of Memory* and chronicled in the film by the same name—is surprisingly poetic, suggesting that in the delicate context of talking about memory, a certain lyricism is difficult to avoid.

The discovery of a biological basis for memory is extremely significant, as is further research that has shown, for instance, how the brain works to suppress unwanted or undesirable memories. This phenomenon is not merely us being consciously selective with our own memories, or a technique in which we manipulate our consciousness; this biological basis of memory tells us that our life experiences become wired into us in deep ways, that our memories are physically transformative and essential features of our selves, and that amnesia has existential consequences. Kandel himself has actually embarked on two life quests, one for this biological basis of memory and the other for his own family history and legacy in prewar and Holocaust-era Vienna. The two quests, the two searches, intertwine to fulfill the telling and prophetic comment by one of Kandel's researchers in the film that given the vastness of possible questions in the world, we are inevitably piqued to ask those questions that connect to who we are and where we come from. The trauma of Kandel's youth stimulates his desire to explore his past, to travel to his roots and his origins—both in prewar Vienna and in the biology laboratory.

So I wonder: can we make a claim about the collective, even in metaphorical terms, that is similarly audacious to the claim Kandel makes about the individual—that certain types of activity can generate a long-term and sustaining collective memory? Even if it could never be verified in a laboratory, we need to ask: what is that work, that activity, that we might undertake to generate long-term memory in our collective? Kandel acknowledges that we do this work of selection and prioritizing in our brain and our memory all the time, both consciously and subconsciously. In describing his harrowing departure from his parents and Vienna for a train and then a ship to the United States, Kandel says, "I've removed all feeling of fear from my mind from that period . . . I've just repressed it, I guess." A key task for our collective is to embrace the idea that we have a greater capacity than we think to do the work of encoding our own memories.

This bridge from the biological-individual to the collective-mythic is not altogether far-fetched. Kandel describes his research as, in some ways, entirely about a search for the biological basis of the motto "Never forget." Survivors do not voluntarily forget their trauma; it is subsequent generations who have to do the work of remembering that which they themselves never knew. I cannot speak to the biological question, but I do know that our colloquial "Never forget" derives from a biblical source; and that the current climate of memory, which repeats this mantra without either contemplating the Jewish system from which it emerged or building the programmatic system that Jewish tradition built around the original commandment, risks falling well short of engendering the long-term memory in the collective that its magnitude demands.

This is our task. I make the arguments in this book by focusing on classical texts and the ways they have been marshaled in the past to deal with the challenges faced by their readers over time. I thus argue implicitly that the raw materials already exist for contemporary readers to be able to make sense of our world, without the need to fabricate new ones.

This effort requires a certain approach that I suspect some readers may be hesitant to make. If we are to find a sympathetic and familiar voice in our tradition and past that we can make usable, we have to be willing to look for it, and we have to read with a sympathetic eye. I find in my teaching that my students are often surprised by classical texts, by how contemporary and aware they seem to be, by how much relevance they bespeak, by how easily they acclimate to pressing issues. Of course I know that as the interpreter and translator I invariably choose texts that will be relevant and applicable from an enormous, inaccessible, and often alienating corpus, and that my teaching methods do much of the bridging work. Still, the outcome is noteworthy: the recognition that space and time do not in and of themselves create a chasm between the old and the new. To demonstrate this connectedness, I engage in a certain *torat hesed* with the past, a loving demeanor that I bring to the texts in the assumption that they will reward that outlook. A skeptical and critical eye might too be surprised by the texts, but would have to work much harder. My friend and teacher Rabbi Ethan Tucker counsels his students to "identify with the Rabbis," to read alongside the texts rather than in inherent confrontation with them. Many moderns would resist this approach simply because of the idiosyncrasies that make the texts alienating, the basic assumptions about theology, gender, human responsibility, and civil discourse that make the rabbis embarrassing rather than a source of pride for contemporary Jews. That we can find or make meaning of the past seems now obvious to me, but I know it requires trust and a commitment to deep learning, as well as a close eye on the learner's personal integrity. My hope is that my approach nurtures these commitments, and that it reinforces Soloveitchik's apt words from the essay we discussed earlier: "Losing confidence in one's own authenticity means losing confidence in one's entitlement to power." The better we are capable of framing a transformative vision in the language of, and with fidelity to, our past, the more authentic the transformative power that will emerge.

In what follows, I offer first my understanding of how Jewish memory works: that most fundamentally Jewish memory is characterized by its relationship to commandedness, to the language of mitzvah. I suggest that this does not necessarily connote a tether to one specific set of obligations per se, but to the culture of what it means to draw from the past in order to dictate how we act in the present. Sensitivity to this core feature of Jewishness—and an understanding of its complexity—helps us unpack how memory classically functioned and achieved its goals.

We then move into mitzvah's core components, spending two chapters on the key motivations that drive a life of commandedness: commandments performed out of yir'ah, or awe; and commandments performed out of ahavah, or love. In both of these chapters we consider the problems associated with assuming these stances as people who dwell in the modern world, as people who struggle with the dogma that we consider axiomatic and that underlies these attitudes. Taken together, these stances lead us to radically consider our place in this world, and to contemplate what it will mean for contemporary Jewry to truly "return" toward the past.

I then explore the most resonant and painful testing-ground for modern Jews on the question of memory, namely how we hold these ideas in balance with the rawness of the recent traumas in

Jewish history—most specifically the Holocaust. Understanding the place of *hurban*, of devastation and destruction, in the construction of Jewish mythic memory, helps us formulate more useful language on how to integrate recent events into our remaking and reclaiming a contemporary lived Judaism. This discussion then leads to the driving goal of the following chapter, on rehabilitating *teshuva*—or repentance—as a contemporary ambition for the Jewish collective.

I conclude the book in two ways: first, I offer an extended analysis of a single classical rabbinic text as a parable for enlightenment and its aftermath, and as a model for how we use the stuff of the Jewish past to liberate and transform the present. Then, I offer more specific programmatic thoughts on how we translate this approach to Jewishness to a contemporary climate rife with anxiety on exactly this memory question.

# CHAPTER 1

# Mitzvah

## MEMORY *as* COMMANDEDNESS

The sanctity of the basic measures of the Torah is the same, whether these units were transmitted to Moses at Sinai or decrees of a court of law, because it is the nation's acceptance that is significant, and it is due to their commitment that we fulfill in purity even matters that are only decrees of later generations.

—*Rabbi Abraham Isaac Kook,*
*Igerot HaReiyah 1.194*

Our first task is to try to come up with a theory of Jewish memory. What does it mean for a people to have memory? How does collective memory interface with the memories that each of us carries around? And once we establish a sense of collective memory, how does it become culturally defining? What classical Jewish ideas about memory help us understand the place of memory in Jewish identity and consciousness?

As we also saw earlier, the emancipation and liberalization of

Judaism had as its great tool the scientific study of Jewish history. The knowledge of history, of the scientific and empirical "real past" that has been obscured by the selectivity of memory, is fundamentally freeing. We also saw earlier how widespread a kind of memory anxiety is in Jewish life—and the awkward ways in which we attempt to "do" memory that seem really quite different from the way memory was classically done.

I suggested earlier that we consider history and memory as characteristics that define kinds of Jewishness—that we are, in a deeper and more essential way, either people of history or people of memory. Perhaps history and memory are not merely tools used to think about the past, or methodological tools in the hands of practitioners, but features of identity that explain how we think about ourselves. Our calendar and its liturgy, and many of our most defining texts, are obsessed with the past, to the point where we might rightly say that thinking about the past constitutes an essentially Jewish act. If so, then, when we think about a shift from memory to history, we may not have merely traded one heuristic tool for another but rather completely altered our collective consciousness. Given the significance of the past and how the past is used, perhaps how we think about the past is not merely a question for the professionals but a reciprocal, personal, and collective question about identity: how does the changing of our past fundamentally change who we are?

Taken differently, we might ask: is it so easy to reconstruct the identity of a broken, demythologized self? The Jewish identity as people of memory effected the community's staying power, its sense of continuity and purposefulness. Again, a fundamental shift in core values may require more than a quick translation of terminology for Jewishness to remain intact.

Herein lies the basic difference between history and memory, and a first step toward helping us define what Jewish memory looks like. The difference between the historical and memorial is not in methodology or in accuracy—for memory can be photographic and memoirs can be precise—but in the reciprocal effects that history and memory have on us. *Where history informs, memory commands.* History enables standing apart, outside, above the past; we learn from its mistakes, we correct misperceptions, we salvage that which is forgotten. The reformers cherished the freedom granted by a knowledge of ancient history not to be bound by that history, or to pursue a different path alluded to in the Jewish past that had been forgotten. They embodied a paradigm wherein history and its attendant categories of empiricism and detachment became, in Yerushalmi's memorable phrase, the faith of fallen Jews.

Memory, meanwhile, whether by design or by accident, wields a commanding force over those who remember. Trauma victims, and anyone who experiences pain and suffering, understand this too well: memories lodge themselves in our consciousness and can be controlling, even debilitating. The processes of therapy and psychoanalysis excavate within our memory, not to surgically remove our memories but to redistribute or reinterpret their commanding impact. Successful therapy can transform and recreate our personal narratives so that we contextualize our suppressed memories and reduce their intrinsic, often-threatening force. Given that therapy essentially consists of rewriting a personal narrative, memories left alone have implicit capacity in forcing a narrative and attendant behaviors all their own.

The idea of commandedness is more complicated in Jewish text and Jewish thought than it is often portrayed. We tend to think of commandedness in the most simple and straightforward terms: God says do X, and we/the Israelites/Moses/Adam or whomever is then supposed to obey. This basic, almost pediatric commandedness originates in the first narrative in the Bible. Immediately after being formed, Adam is given a set of instructions: eat this but not that! And as if to suggest disobedience is intrinsic to the human condition, Adam cannot help violating the one rule that if only followed would yield an everlasting lifetime in paradise. We smile when reading this story, seeing our own children: the temptation created around this literal and mythical forbidden fruit is simply too much to bear. No other fruit comes close to the appeal of that from which we are kept at arm's length. But we must also note that built into this pediatric, "imposed" commandedness is a basic problem:

God warns Adam not to eat the fruit, for if he should do so, he will certainly die. Adam violates the rule but does not meet this fate. There is no better way to undermine a command than in failing to follow through in the consequences. Indeed, Adam does ultimately lose the potentiality for immortality; but that is a far stretch from what seemed like the inevitable consequence suggested by the original commandment. Without the immediate punitive consequences, we wonder: was death really an inevitable outcome? Was this the kind of commandment that was ordered for Adam's own good, or an exercise in divine power for the purpose of establishing authority? After all, if Adam does not yet know good from evil, how can he know to disobey?

The covenantal theology underlying this version of commandedness is neatly expressed in the Torat Kohanim, the rabbinic midrash on Leviticus (9:12). Commenting on the verse "You shall be holy to Me, for I the LORD am holy, and I have set you apart from other peoples to be Mine" (Leviticus 20:26), the rabbis pick up on the unusual phrasing: Holiness here is not a state that appears to have independent merit. The text implies that we become holy and do things to achieve this state of holiness only because God too is holy. Achieving holiness is a technique of imitatio dei, of imitating God. In their commentary, the rabbis say as follows:

> Rabbi Elazar ben Azaryah said: From where do we know that a person should not say, "I have no desire to wear clothes made of wool and linen, I have no desire to eat the meat of pigs, I have no desire to commit adultery." Rather, a person should say, "I desire [these things]; but what can I do? My father in heaven forbids it."

Commandedness, here, is an act of subjugation to a will that exceeds ours: it is functionally equivalent to obedience, made more forceful by Rabbi Elazar's demand that we particularly subject ourselves to God's will with respect to those things we most covet and want. Real commandedness, then, is manifest most when it goes against our will and instinct.

But this model of imposed commandedness—do this, or else! —is not our only option in understanding Jewish responsibility. A number of our classic texts on commandedness interweave memory, narration, and personal ownership into the very process of how we integrate the commands incumbent upon us. In Exodus 12:51, God instructs Moses to command the Israelites to consecrate the firstborns, both the humans and the animals. What does "consecrate" mean? Taken alone, it is hard to say. Does God mean to now exact retribution, or perhaps payment, from the freed Israelites, seeing their freedom as dependent on the death of the firstborns of the Egyptians? The commandment seems dangerously ambiguous. And so Moses, rather remarkably, *translates* the commandment not just into a viable morality for the Israelites—sacrifice the animals, redeem the children—but he does so through a careful and programmatic narration of the Exodus story, as part of a long list of other commandments that do not seem to be part of God's original command, and most important, opens his "repetition" of God's words to the Israelites with the phrase: remember. Memory is a tool of commandedness; when we actually remember, commanding power naturally flows.

Two powerful rabbinic teachings, woven together, apply this truth of individual scientific and behavioral memory to the Jewish collective. The Talmud famously teaches in Tractate *Niddah* (30b) the myth that the fetus is taught the entire Torah in utero, only to be struck by an angel upon entry to the world and made, in the Talmud's language, to forget it all. In this rabbinic teaching—perhaps meant as a version of the Socratic method—life becomes a process of reclaiming that which we once knew. A life of learning is not marked by an accumulation of wisdom or a collection of knowledge, but a recalling to mind that which has been forgotten. How striking it is that this teaching comes from the elite learned class, those privileged by educational opportunities and capable of using their accumulated knowledge to wield authority over others! Wouldn't the rabbis seem more likely to preach the opposite model, in which knowledge comes in storehouses to which they hold the key? No, in the rabbis' understanding of the world, there is no single piece of wisdom, no keys to the kingdom that have not already been possessed at one time or another by even the lowliest and most ignorant. The rabbis and the learned then become less teachers of

Torah, and certainly not controllers of Torah, and more therapists and memory-joggers, helping us to remember that which we already know.

In Tractate *Shavuot* (5a) the rabbis discuss infants again—but this time in a legal context, focusing on those infants born into environments where they might never learn to remember. The *tinok she'nishba*—the captive infant—provides a perfect example to test this hypothesis on knowledge as essentially memory, and the bridge between memory and obligation. An infant born into an environment wherein he never learns about the obligations attendant on him cannot be held liable. Obligations are not intrinsic to Jewishness; they are contingent on the memory of the original command. The rabbis expand on this idea in Tractate *Shabbat* (68a), where they rule that liability for transgressive behavior is contingent on memory of the law: a person who forgets the essence of Shabbat and sins by violating Shabbat over and over is only liable for one offense, the one sin of forgetting. This stands in stark contrast to the Latin principle that underlies our contemporary judicial system, the principle "Ignorantia juris non excusat"—ignorance of the law is not an excuse for its transgression. To the rabbis, this is the only imaginable excuse—knowledge, memory, and commandedness are so deeply intertwined that a person who forgets his or her obligations is exonerated, albeit with some sadness about the social and cultural ramifications of this particular kind of amnesia.

History liberates while memory obligates. The revelation at Sinai including the giving over of the Decalogue is recorded twice in the Torah—in Exodus and Deuteronomy. To the consternation of many commentators, the commandment regarding Shabbat uses different imperatives in the two places: in Exodus, we are commanded to remember—*Zakhor*; in Deuteronomy, to guard or observe—*Shamor*. In Tractate *Shavuot* (20b) the rabbis seek to resolve this problem not by modern biblical critical methods but through citing an earlier rabbinic mystical teaching according to which the two commandments—*Zakhor* and *Shamor*—emerged in the same incomprehensible divine utterance. At the source of this teaching in the midrashic tradition, *Zakhor* and *Shamor* are cast as not merely opposite; they are presented as *contradictory* and as such are listed together with several other biblical laws that on first glance appear to be at odds with each other. The broader theological lesson of the passage is that God and God alone can speak two opposite teachings in the same breath, and thus what we as humans perceive as internal contradictions in the Bible merely reflect our own failings—and not a divine error. As we shall see, this is a key example in a larger lesson for us to explore about the aspiration to exist within dissonance—to find ways to co-inhabit contradictory realities without needing to suppress one or the other.

The implication for this discussion of this particular example, however, especially as it is mediated by some of the medieval commentators, is that the rabbis link memory to commandedness as essential features that validate even as they may contradict each other. Shamor, on its own, is defensive and fearful; Zakhor, alone, is powerless. There can be no memory without commandment, and no commandment without memory.

But the most profound expression of the theology of memory, with the deepest ramifications for how memory factors into Jewish peoplehood, is expressed in a different rabbinic teaching. In the homiletic Midrash Tanhuma (Pekudei 3), the rabbis imagine that all Jewish souls, past and present, stood at the receiving of the Torah and the conferral of its obligations at Sinai, and assented aloud to its commitments with the memorable phrase from Exodus that "all that God spoke, we shall do!" It is difficult to overstate how radical this idea truly is, that future converts to the Jewish people do not enter the covenant at the moment they emerge from the mikvah but rather that they reclaim a retroactive participation at Sinai: they merely now, for the first time, remember that core experience and assume its attendant obligations. Converts are not outsiders, lower on a hierarchy; ethnicity and background have little value in this system. Once you enter and accept the system, you can flip a switch and assume a suppressed memory.

This stance is even more radical when compared with the different route taken by other Jews in the ancient world, those who followed the teachings of the apostle Paul. The classical rabbis and the early Christians found themselves responding to the same core problem—a problem that echoes our current reality—the confrontation between the redemptive myth of Israel and the ruptures that their modernity had wrought—whether in the devastating fate suffered in the destruction of the Temple and the covenantal narrative or in the more subtle existential challenges brought about by cultural and political opportunity. Their responses split along exactly this issue.

In the eleventh chapter of the Letter to the Romans, Paul discusses the challenge of bringing in new people—gentile Christians—to the covenantal narrative of the Jewish people to which Jesus belongs, and which Jesus has come to transform. Paul needs to revise the Jewish particularistic narrative—the story of a particular people—to allow for the inclusion of outsiders in what is becoming a universal mission. He therefore metaphorically describes the Jewish covenantal narrative as a tree. The tree trunk is the lineage of Israelite history, and the tree branches are contemporary Jews and Christians. Some branches are natural outgrowths, and some are grafted on. The failure of the Jews to properly bloom in Christ may result in them snapping off the tree, while faith in Christ enables gentile Christians to graft themselves to the tree and thus to bloom. The entry of gentile Christians into the covenant is historical—it happens at a moment in time, with a marked point of entry. Christ does not merely transform the covenant; he terminates it. Christianity is fundamentally historical: it exists within the parameters of past time as succeeded by present time. Hence Paul uses terms like adoption, whereby Christians become heirs to the parent-child covenant despite their late entry to the family, and grafting, as in our example, whereby a species is propagated through the introduction of a genetically different component.

Paul sees this rupture, the introduction of history to the narrative of Jewish destiny, as the opening that he needs to build a bridge from the particular narrative of the Jewish people to the human and universal story of the world. Adoption becomes the language by which the particularistic narrative is translated to a universal mission. Paul does not altogether jettison the ethnic bond of Israel, as Israel still constitutes the tree trunk; but he fundamentally historicizes the Israelite covenant. It *was* at one point in time; it has been *altered* due to the confrontations of the first century; it *perpetuates* now not just for Israel but for all those who will join.

The rabbis wrestled with the same basic theological and infrastructural challenge. As we know, part of their response entailed creating an interpretive approach to history so that, as opposed to Paul, they might imagine for themselves and for their descendants the continuity of the Jewish mythic covenantal narrative. The rabbis, on the whole, transform the history they lived—including its unimaginable cataclysms—to constitute a continuation of the mythic superstructure that they inherited. This is not the departure from history, or a rejection of history, as much as a rerouting of the challenge that history presents: myth and memory are a means of owning history rather than being rebuked by it.

But the rabbis also created their own new theology to respond to the universalist challenge. Although the rabbis did not throw open the doors to Jewishness and instead created a specific ritual of conversion to control the point of entry, they simultaneously offered this teaching that all Jews were present at the revelation at Sinai. This means not only those who were actually incarnate at Sinai, not merely their descendants who inherit the ethnic-covenantal bond, but even all the converts who are destined to join the Jewish people. The rabbis' tree metaphor would look totally different: converts become *part of the trunk* itself, not newly grafted branches. The message for Jewish mythic memory is also extraordinary: our mythic memory is not an ethnically contingent set of experiences from which we grow distant as time passes from the actual Sinai revelation, but something inherent to even our contemporary Jewishness. We too stood at Sinai, alongside the ancient Israelites who may have historically actually been there; our memory of the experience is equally firsthand. Our recollection is not the product of storytelling but of our innate experience of the divine—as it is simultaneously both rooted in our consciousness and acquirable by those who enter our ranks.

In the same Talmudic passage that places converts at Sinai, we find the famous rabbinic dictum *Kol Israel arevim zo b'zo*—colloquially translated to mean that "all Jews are responsible for one another."

The word *arevim* is part of the technical vocabulary of bondsmen and guarantors. The responsibility that the text suggests is legally specific—not watered down or arbitrary. We are all *guarantors*, co-signers, for one another, since we witnessed and agreed to the same covenant. We therefore take a high level of responsibility, we maintain accountability, for the debts and obligations we have incurred as part of our commitment, together, once upon a time, at the foot of Mount Sinai. If others opt out, we owe the debt. Willful amnesia is actually criminal and destructive of the social order.

What is so telling about this teaching is that the rabbis place this moment of collective memory, the original founding moment in our memory as Jews, specifically at the foot of Sinai. There were other options: we might find ourselves laughing with Abraham and Sarah as they learned of their future as centenarian parents of an heir to their name; or wailing in agony under the taskmasters' whips in Egypt; or marveling in what we can only imagine as stunned silence as the waters of the Red Sea parted upon the solitary leap of faith of Nahshon, son of Aminadav, into their swollen currents; or even looking across the Jordan at the Promised Land as it unfolded before their eyes. All these moments could have served as the original anchor for the sense of peoplehood embodied in this constructed collective memory. Instead, the rabbis located our formative memory at Sinai, the place not merely of revelation but of our binding commitment to a covenant to the Torah, the place of our wedding canopy with the divine and all the rights and responsibilities that came along with that union. Sinai is the site of commandment and commitment; our core memory of peoplehood is intertwined deeply with *mitzvah*. Not merely liberation, not merely the building of a nation—but the sense of having been commanded, and having accepted that charge. Or more accurately, given the curious phraseology in the text of Exodus, it is the site of having accepted the onus of commandment even prior to the issuance of the command itself. As Jon Levenson writes beautifully in his *Sinai and Zion*, Sinai symbolizes the moment at which the Torah's narrative ends and is replaced by a covenantal relationship defined by responsibility—and which we know becomes a relationship in which we are freely capable of proactively defining and *redefining* those responsibilities. In contrast to the message of Paul's Christ, who comes to replace the law, Sinai is the intersection of love and law, of gift and demand, the link between a past together and a future together. Or in the language of this chapter: Sinai replaces history with a relatable memory and its attendant commanding behaviors.

In their moment of ancient crisis, in the encounter between the particular and the universal, the rabbis might have pursued two all-too-familiar extreme paths. They might have facilitated an inward turn, rejecting the universalist critique and the burden of history altogether. They also might have accepted the universalist critique and the turn to history in radically abandoning the unique particularistic Jewish collective. The rabbis, instead, crafted a theology of deep memory that is capable of stretching across ethnicity; they generated a particularism capable of overriding the limited categories of race and ethnicity as a more viable, long-lasting definition of the collective. And they wrote the acquisition of memory into the conditions for becoming part of the collective, just as they rooted that memory in the covenantal context of commandedness.

The encounters with emancipation and openness in modernity, with the demise of the security of an intrinsic collective, are not new to our collective mythical experience—although we tend to think we are living in unprecedented times. These encounters are already written into our deep mythical memory, starting with the core narrative at the beginning of the book of Genesis. Is there a more obvious parallel to the twin challenges of enlightenment and emancipation than the consuming of the fruit of the tree of knowledge and the resulting expulsion from the Garden of Eden? It is as though the Torah is teaching that the entirety of our tradition stems from a need to respond to these twin challenges, that all the mythic narratives that tell the story of the emergence of the collective people Israel, the entirety of our particularism, come as an active response to the universalist challenge.

It may be, though, that we misread one key element of the Eden story. The story of the tree of knowledge implies that discovery and disobedience are intrinsically linked, that the moment of enlightenment brings with it the inevitable and thus legitimate impulse to flee from commandedness—or worse, that enlightenment alone is a fundamental act of rebellion. Were that the case, should not Adam and Eve have died upon eating the fruit (as they were warned would happen)? Or perhaps God should have brought about the deluge as punishment for this disobedient act now, rather than generations and chapters later, to send this clear message. Instead, the consistent element characterizes the divine-human relationship both *before* and *after* Adam and Eve eat of the fruit of the tree—they remain in a commanded-covenantal relationship. The rules are stricter afterward, and the existence is more challenging. But the challenges of wisdom and enlightenment, be they existential malaise, spiritual boredom, insatiable intellectual curiosity—are these not small prices to pay for the gifts of knowledge and awareness?

This crisis and its subsequent moments of critical choice have reappeared mythically and metaphorically throughout Jewish history, and the choices before us have precedent. In the turmoil of the first century, the matrix from which rabbinic Judaism was born, ancient Jews looked in one direction and saw the inviting, open porticos to the transformative world of Greek philosophy and wisdom. In the other direction lay the burning embers of the Jerusalem temple, God's footstool, the centripetal force of their particularism, and with it the collapse of their religious system. To mediate and navigate their way out, the rabbis crafted a system to bind themselves to a mythical metanarrative rooted in a selective memory of the past, in which they played a central role and from which they radically and progressively transformed their core culture and value systems. Modern Jews face a comparable dual challenge in the existential threats of openness and closure; and we are challenged to come up with an equally tenable and lasting answer. How do we place ourselves back in a covenantal, commanding relationship to the past, to our core memories, such that we become liberated by this authenticity to radically revision our future?

For all their mythic attachment to the past—in fact, due to it—the rabbis also served as perhaps the most radical and transformative change-agents Jewish history has ever seen. Memory, in the hands of the rabbis, became the tool by which they granted themselves the authenticity they needed to paradoxically reimagine the present. The rabbis used a now-notorious idea known as *yeridat ha-*

*dorot*—the decline of the generations—to situate themselves in a chain of tradition. This idea tends to be read as a self-deprecating depiction of inferiority, culturally comparable to the somewhat grating tendency of people, as they get older, to complain that things are not what they used to be. Young people, in turn, are apt to resent this notion that they are incapable of achieving what their forbears did, especially since everything we know about evolution and about the accumulation of wisdom suggests that standing on the shoulders of our predecessors should enable us to see farther and achieve more than they ever did.

But placing ourselves within a chain need not be a route to self-deprecation. The great medieval innovator Moses Maimonides was capable of integrating the importance of dwelling within a long-standing tradition with a healthy sense of self-importance. "From Moses to Moses"—from the biblical prophet to Maimonides— "none arose quite like Moses." In one fell swoop, Maimonides claims authority together with a fidelity to at least this one predecessor. The mythic chain of tradition is precisely the tool with which authenticity is created—in the ability to occupy a role in a mythic history, in the use of mythic language —as the empowering framework that allows for innovation to flower. When the rhetoric of personal autonomy is allowed to rule, we are left to transmit to those who follow us only a story that starts with us, sealing with frightening permanence the ruptures we make in our relationship to our received tradition, to what we grow up with, that we imagine must begin with our own lives. It is lonely at the top of the evolutionary chain, and even on the shoulders of others—especially when we fail to look down. When all that lies below is history, then that history—to borrow Jung's terminology—disappears beneath the modern man into primeval mist.

The rhetoric of "continuity" that dominates the American Jewish landscape has this exact blind spot, encapsulated in its very use of a term that connotes passivity. Instead of speaking about the transmission of values or ideas from one generation to the next, we use this awkward gerund—"continuity"—that suggests our hope that a subsequent generation follows in some ways in our footsteps. The late political philosopher Daniel Elazar outlined five key areas for the work of Jewish continuity—Torah, Am Yisrael (peoplehood), Klal Yisrael (pluralism), Berit (covenant), and Kiruv (outreach.) In the current climate, continuity is essentially a euphemism merely for Berit—for the concern that Jewish ethnic particularism is losing out to the assimilative forces of universalism. The problem with this metonym is that it constitutes a basic laziness—rather than saying what we want to say, or conveying the values we care about, we harp with anxiety on a problem that is overtaking us as we watch passively.

The framework of memory and its cultivation, meanwhile, offers a different template: it demands on one hand the active, transhistorical willingness to accept and own the burden of the past, and on the other hand offers the liberating possibility of authentically transforming that past legacy in the image of the present. Classical rabbinic literature has two key terms for the transmission of ideas and information from one generation to the next—masoret, which is the active work of transmitting, and kabbalah, which is the equally active work of receiving. These terms are best encapsulated in the first teaching in the first chapter of Mishnah Avot, in the ideal example of a rabbinic cosmogonic myth: Moses received (kbl) the Torah at Sinai, transmitted it (msr) to the elders, and within but one chapter it has reached rabbis contemporary to the writing of the text itself. Lost in this memory text—and deliberately so—are the architectural elements that would make it historical and mark the passage of time. But preserved in this narrative, in the epigrams that mark the receipt and transmission of the Torah, is the deeply creative impulse that makes the very Torah being transmitted evolve before our very eyes. It is in the ownership of each succeeding rabbi, marked by the work of his teacher in transmitting and his own work of receiving, owning, and then passing along, that the bridging between past legacy, present responsibility, and future transformation takes place.

So this memory that I am talking about is not nostalgia or romanticism. Memory does not involve aspiring to live in the past but aspiring for an actively constructed and interpreted continuity between what we take from the past, who we are in the present, and what we convey to the future.

And I am also not limiting the language of commandedness to

mean the conditioning of behaviors specific to one mode of Jewish religious practice. The rabbis teach that greater is the one who is commanded and obeys the command than the one who performs the same deed voluntarily. This conflicts with our commonly held conviction that good behaviors offered freely, without compulsion, are superior to obedience. I think the rabbis teach us a different ethical value: when we alone are the arbiters of our Jewishness, when will we ever find the fulfillment of completing our task? Purposefulness requires the sense of obedience to a command, regardless of the commander.

For memory to generate purposefulness, it must entail using the past in our production of myth and in our use of language so that we might make meaning that is relevant to the present. The ritualized storytelling of Purim and Passover empowers each generation of Jews to feel as though our memory of these past events is as valid as that of those who came before, even if it is influenced by our selective priorities and needs. Memory at Passover becomes an exercise in accumulating layers, as we remember both the core Exodus together with our memories of our own Passovers past. Passover as it is liturgized and celebrated unites past, present, and future. Indeed, whenever the Torah uses the language of *Zakhor*, whenever it commands that we remember or, perhaps more accurately, that we "recall," it is commanding not the passive exercise that we usually associate with memory—the attempt to desperately cling to that which we once knew better—but an active behavioral task. It is not enough, says the medieval commentator Nahmanides, to remember Amalek in our hearts, nor even to recite a prescribed liturgy of memory. Only when we recount to our children and our children's children, in a language we know and a context we understand, do we generate the memory that our past commands.

It seems to me that the crisis of memory that we speak about in Jewish life lies first in a confusion of what memory really means, and in the dangerous irony that we tend to confuse memory with history. Memory—or at least Jewish memory—is not a photographic, comprehensive catalog. Jewish memory privileges distance from the event so long as the creative recreation of the memory comes with a sense of commandedness, a commitment to the obligations that stem from the selective memory. The generation of Israelites who watched revelation and lived through redemption were themselves unable to also transition to becoming the people who would enter the Promised Land. If both the exciting and traumatic elements of modernity have brought us also a measure of brokenness, must we accept this fate? Must we accede to the assumption that our memory cannot be rehabilitated, for all the capacity it may have to invigorate and stimulate newness in Jewish life?

The memory I am talking about is the kind evoked by Marcus Hansen, the historian of immigration, who wrote in 1938 that "what the son wishes to forget the grandson wishes to remember." Hansen looks at three generations—the pioneers, their struggling children who seek to forget, and the third generation that comes along and self-consciously asks, "This property is our achievement, that of myself and of my fathers; it is a sign of the hardy stock from which we have sprung; who were they and why did they come?" This set of questions is premised on a self-awareness and a desire to see a linkage between past and present, not to stand above or beyond the past but precisely to stand in relationship to it—to understand the ways in which our heritage implicates and obligates our present. In Tractate Sotah (13a) the Talmudic rabbis weave an extraordinary tale about Jacob's burial in the cave of Machpela: Esau came to block the entry of the funeral procession, claiming his own right to the plot. He and the procession members argued and debated the legal merits, and ultimately Jacob's son Naftali—described biblically as fleet of foot—was dispatched back to Egypt to fetch the legal documents that would indicate Jacob's ownership of the birthright and its attendant rights of burial. Hushim son of Dan—Jacob's deaf grandson—could not follow the proceedings, but when they were explained to him, he became incensed that his grandfather would suffer the indignity of lying unburied while the issue was sorted out. He crushed Esau's head, and the funeral proceeded.

Hushim represents the fulfillment of a thread started by Jacob himself in the biblical narrative. Earlier, Jacob had carried on the tradition of passing on the Abrahamic blessing—but actually skipped his son (Joseph) and instead blessed his own grandsons. In doing so, Jacob makes explicit what the Bible had previously conveyed subtly about Isaac—that these blessings flow from son to son, but are fulfilled most deeply in alternating generations. Hushim stands and watches the legal wrangling that comes with legacy, but implicitly understands that the power of memory lies in its moral obligations that transcend the direct line of transmission. Hushim acts purposefully and with conviction, and in doing so fulfills Jacob's legacy more effectively than his father or uncles ever could. His deafness becomes essential to the metaphor, as he inherits less of the literal stuff of transmission than of the underlying ethic of behavior.

The notion that history replaces or supersedes memory sells short memory's radically transformative capabilities. So too does the fixation on accuracy and veracity as the authentic measures of memory. What has distinguished Jewish memory has been its relationship to the burden of commandment, obligation, and responsibility as an ethical stance toward the world: when we forget who we are, we know not what we are supposed to be doing, and I suppose the opposite is true as well. When God in the Bible is described as remembering—whether vis-à-vis the patriarchs or the suffering of the Israelites under the burden of slavery—the verb is used to introduce not just the revival of the covenantal relationship but the reentry of God into history as active participant, a reassertion of divine responsibility. How will our remembering manifest itself?

Before we consider this question, we must think more about the mechanics of how we as moderns are to work with this category and its assumptions. If we can now assume the relationship between memory and mitzvah, let us consider the components of mitzvah next. What does Jewish commandedness consist of, and how are those impulses aligned with our sensibilities?

# CHAPTER 2

# Yir'ah

## AWE *as* INQUIRY *and* DISCERNMENT

> To return to Saint Edmund Campion's last days: at the
> very close of his interrogation, his questioners tried to
> get him to deny the real presence, to which Campion
> replied, "What? Will you make [Christ] a prisoner now
> in Heaven? . . . Heaven is his palace and you will make
> it his prison." We might ask the same of historicism
> and the discourses of modernity. Must they make of
> their critical frameworks a prison of presence? Or can
> we find in the languages of modern critical inquiry
> a way to understand the power and reality in history
> and culture of real presence?
>
> —Robert Orsi, "When 2 + 2 = 5"

In examining the essential relationship between memory and mitzvah, we considered how we recount the events of our collective and
mythical past and what obligations become attendant upon us with
that recollection. Memory is always selective and at the same time

always commanding; thus we can self-consciously and deliberately choose to once again become people of memory and in turn people of obligation.

But what does it mean to actually take on this sense of commandedness? What does it offer to our contemporary, modern, enlightened Jewishness, which is likely not interested in moving or prepared to move backward in time or in consciousness in order to assume this mantle? In what ways do commandment, obligation, and responsibility help bridge the past to the present without undermining it?

In classical Jewish thought, there are essentially two motivating impulses for the commandments: commandments are performed out of love, *ahavah*, or out of awe or fear, *yir'ah*. To love God and to fear God are also considered freestanding independent commandments by Maimonides and some of the other cataloguers of such lists; but as part of unpacking the underlying attitudes of the commanded self, the rabbis debate whether it is better to act out of love or to act out of awe or fear. Ultimately, of course, the most convincing of such debates are those that are resolved by recognizing that each of these motivations expresses something convincing, authentic, and true; and that the human spirit requires both impulses. We will explore both in turn, but first we examine "awe." What does it mean to obey out of awe or fear? Why would we want to do such a thing? What in our world is deserving of such awe, and genuinely awe-inspiring? What if we are not really afraid of anything?

Once again the calendar is a useful starting point. The same Jewish liturgical calendar that features a memory season from Purim to the Ninth of Av then gives way to what we might call "awe" season. The Yamim Noraim, the Days of Awe, run from Rosh HaShanah through the following month or so of feasts and fasts. As with the holidays of memory, the Days of Awe have their own particular stage direction, rituals, and costuming that help ramp up the palpable and corporeal sense of awesomeness—the traditional white attire, the haunting melodies, and a liturgy that emphasizes the tenuous line between life and death. And as with memory season, all this drama and architecture embodies a powerful ideology that we are remiss not to take seriously. Most suggestive in this respect is that Rosh HaShanah is both a day of awe and, in biblical language, Yom HaZikaron—Memorial Day. The architecture of the day intends to bring about an experience of awe as an essential component of memory.

And what is this "awe"? In the tenth chapter of Deuteronomy, after Moses recapitulates the historical drama of the giving of the Torah in the wilderness, he states with stunning clarity what it is that God wants. In a one-sentence encapsulation of biblical religion, Moses says:

> And now, O Israel, what does the LORD your God demand of you? Only this—to revere the LORD your God, to walk only in His paths, to love Him, and to serve the LORD your God with all your heart and soul, keeping the LORD commandments and laws, which I enjoin upon you today, for your good.

Rarely are the lessons of the Torah so straightforward; usually devotees spend their lives' energy searching for the right formula of behaviors and beliefs to appease God and find fulfillment. And yet here Moses spells out God's wishes in the clear, with a list of four obligations: to revere, l'yirah; to love; to walk in His path; and to serve the LORD through observing the commandments. There are two basic ways to interpret the sentence. The structure can be read as a list of four separate obligations, which would suggest that perhaps yir'ah comes first but is not intrinsically more valuable. Alternatively, we can read the word yir'ah as the direct object of the command, after which the remainder of the sentence—the rest of the commands—is subordinate and explanatory. The interpretation depends a bit on how you punctuate the sentence.

In either reading, at the core of Jewish obligation stands the reverence of God. In both our literary and liturgical traditions, this experience of awe lies at the heart of what it means to be commanded. So what does it mean to revere, or to stand in awe—either of God, as in this case, or, for that matter, of anything?

The Hebrew word at the root of this obligation is the verb l'yirah. In the Torah, sometimes the word yir'ah can be translated to mean "fear"—as when God commands Abraham that he not fear, for

God will stay with him. But in other cases, as in here in Deuteronomy, translating yir'ah simply as fear—as a freestanding commandment to fear God—makes less sense. In this context, just prior to this commandment, God is pleading with the people of Israel that they recall what they have seen with their own eyes, and that they see the potential blessings and curses that lie before them on the basis of whether they choose to do what God has asked. This biblical context, linking "seeing" to "standing in awe," evokes the tantalizing but elusive relationship between the word yir'ah and the Hebrew verb ra'ah, from the verb "to see." These words clearly sound alike, as though they constitute the active and passive forms of the same verb.

So a translation of the word yir'ah that may best capture this connotation, of a specific kind of seeing that accords value and esteem to the seen, is "to hold the LORD your God in awe." Even in English this phrase lends the sense of a phenomenon that transcends mere seeing—a kind of voluntary beholding, wherein we see something beyond the visible, as we say idiomatically when we talk about truly seeing something for the first time.

The Torah, then, is implicitly linking these two issues, demanding that the people of Israel remember what they have seen with their own eyes, and then commanding them to stand in awe of God. In doing so, the Torah suggests—I think problematically—that this awe is fundamentally contingent on the seeing. This brings to mind the commonplace but problematic understanding of memory as an ever-fading negative image that is preserved in the mind, to which we desperately cling and try to recall. Here too, the contingency of yir'ah on atem re'item—you have seen—as God says to the people of Israel after the awe-inspiring Exodus from Egypt, suggests that that awe risks becoming diminished with the passing of time, with the fading of memory. It also suggests that this awe can be difficult to acquire and virtually impossible to transmit, thus removing the power of human agency.

The problems should be obvious. If something is in and of itself truly awe-inspiring—the revelation at Sinai, let's say, or an epiphany on the road to Damascus or the gates to the Emerald City—then the awe that emerges is essentially automatic, not freely given or the product of the work that being pious should entail. It is difficult to transmit to others the sensory experience at the core of the commandment, and so the experience invariably wanes. And the worse problem is that in the deepest sense, seeing should be the *opposite* of believing. If I only believe that which I can verify having seen or, in our case, if I only find awesome that which is in and of itself truly and objectively awesome, then God's core commandment is to merely be a receptacle to revelation.

One classic rabbinic response used to explain this text in Deuteronomy—and to expand its obligation far beyond the limited scope that the context seems to imply—is to cite a famous teaching attributed to Rabbi Hanina that appears in several Talmudic texts: "Everything is in the hands of heaven save for the awe of heaven." In one such Talmudic context, in Tractate *Niddah* (16b), this teaching is brought about as the theoretical justification for the myth that the angel who oversees conception brings the drop of semen before God and asks about its fate: Will the baby born of this drop be strong or weak? Rich or poor? Wise or foolish? But the angel does not ask whether the person will be righteous or wicked—for, as R. Hanina teaches, everything is in the hands of heaven save for the awe of heaven! In other words, God can take care of the externalities, the peripheral components of the natural world and human life, but the one thing God cannot control is human free will. By linking this teaching to the verse in Deuteronomy, these commentators dramatically expand that original commandment. Rather than a freestanding obligation to stand in awe of God, we are commanded to exercise our free will correctly in choosing righteousness. The commandment becomes so much bigger, almost hopelessly all-encompassing.

This understanding of the verse in Deuteronomy also essentially distills a particular commandment to the Israelite people into the basic core principle of all religious life. Consider this problematic analogy that emerges from taking "awe" and turning it into free will. In his doctrine of justification by faith alone, Martin Luther maintained that the one essential act humans are able to undertake is that of faith in Christ, which can then unlock the outpouring of grace that comes from God alone. The believer humbles himself into a receptacle in the face of God, committing the selfless act of faith and receiving grace in the process. When awe becomes and a stand-in for a single positive exercise of free will, it risks losing all its particularistic power.

I suppose the Talmud and the medieval Jewish commentators who provide this explanation would resist this analogy to Luther for a variety of reasons. Maimonides, for one, subordinates awe as inferior to steps that the pious must take and that manifest *ahavah*, or love. For Luther, faith is the only fundamentally necessary step; for Maimonides and traditional Jewish thought, awe may begin the process of ascent, but it does not alone create the reciprocal divine-human relationship. Jewish tradition insists on the performance of commandments as a means of deepening and making manifest our relationship with God. Free will has to be accompanied by a set of responsibilities: most matters are in the hands of heaven, but that does not absolve Jews of ongoing responsibilities embodied in the commandments.

Still, the peril that this *basic* commandment, this prerequisite to commandedness in general, will become *merely* a restatement of free will is strong, as is the peril that it undermines the possibility that the Torah is teaching a more specific lesson by conveying this obligation to stand in awe.

And the real problem with the mandate to stand in awe, why it conflicts with our experience as Jews in the modern age, is not that we continually see and experience revelation and do not know how to hold on to that sense of awe—would that we were so lucky! Nor, I think, is the problem our failure to pay proper attention to what is around us or that we are looking in the wrong places for inspiration. The problem is the opposite. We see everything, and we value our sight enormously; and our ever-growing visual acumen is making what we see less and less awe-inspiring. Many languages, including Hebrew and ancient Greek—which together form the cultural matrix out of which our Judaism is born—conflate the verbs "to see" and "to understand." In the second chapter of Mishnah Avot Rabbi Yohanan ben Zakkai asks his five disciples to go out and see—literally, *tze'u u're'u*—what is the best attribute by which a person should live. After he hears their answers, he responds, "I see the words of Rabbi Elazar b. Arakh over all else, for your answers are all embedded in his answer." Linguists call this phenomenon of conflation the mapping of a metaphor across domains; but at play here is something that may be more than "merely" language. In the third chapter of Genesis, as the serpent rightly predicts, eating of the fruit of knowledge literally opens Adam and Eve's eyes, wherein they "see for the first time." Seeing then is not exactly believing; real seeing—the seeing that comes with enlightenment, with probing and inquisitive eyes—is *understanding*.

The deepest challenge of post-Enlightenment modernity for Jews, I think, lies in this distinction: that the act of stepping forward and seeing things for the first time—be they God, the Torah, ourselves and our community; be they divine, mythical, or holy—with the benefit of our increasingly sharp and penetrating eyes—does not alone, and *will not alone*, generate the reflexive awe that this interpretation of the Torah demands. There is nothing so perfect that cannot be dissected by the microscope, nor so lofty in the heavens that a telescope cannot change it from celestial to concrete. Professor Robert Orsi writes of seeking "a radical empiricism of the visible *and invisible real*" [emphasis in original]—are we capable of seeing this in our narrowing gaze?

Let me take this a bit deeper by using a metaphor employed by the philosopher of religion Wayne Proudfoot: imagine walking in a forest and encountering a bear. The encounter—the seeing—produces a sensation of fear or amazement. Now say that upon looking closer you discover that the bear is actually a fallen log. As the visual image gives way, the original fear and amazement diminishes as well—even though, at the time, that very fear and amazement was a deeply authentic, instinctual response.

In context, scholars use this metaphor to critique the tendency of outsiders watching a religious experience to reduce it to what they see rather than describing the experience as it is lived by the believer. If we watch someone worship a log, we may know cognitively that the person is worshipping a log; but to describe the experience fully and authentically would require positing that the person is actually worshipping a deity. Otherwise the authenticity of the experience is washed over and reduced by the description of the observer.

Let us consider a further implication of this metaphor. If fear and amazement stem from a particular belief about what it is we are seeing, then the clarity that comes when the image sharpens threatens to undermine not only the image itself but also the deeply authentic reaction or response that was stirred in seeing the image in the first place. Since we are inclined to value our sight and inquiry as our arbiters of value, then true discovery has two related but ultimately separate implications: it stands to undermine what it is we see, and it stands to undermine that which we may have experienced prior to fully seeing. It then becomes extraordinarily difficult to command that others continue to express an innate, internally felt sense of awe and amazement after the image has been unmasked.

Achieving a sense of awe—especially a commanded sense of awe—is notoriously difficult. It is especially difficult to stand in awe of those things that our increasingly discerning eyes have made less estimable. We are enlightened and therefore inquisitive, and our gaze is penetrating; and we have also shortened the distance between seeing and understanding with our proliferation of words and expressions that describe and thus categorize and qualify everything. This "processing" is a major component of how we learn; thus the idea that we should stand in awe as an innate experience of the world, that we could continue to experience a silent passivity as an essential and primordial element of life, feels anachronistic and inauthentic.

Indeed, seeing and understanding are neither merely sensory experiences nor neutral encounters. The understanding and the knowing that come with real seeing entail a discourse of power and control. The power of the seer and the vulnerability of the seen are always twinned; the seer wields tremendous force and power over what is seen, with the capacity and tendency to evaluate as quickly as interpret. If our inquiry has made us smarter, it has also empowered us.

What's more, as Abraham Joshua Heschel has demanded, the awe and reverence described in our core texts is not correctly captured in simply standing in awe of nature itself—as though standing by a waterfall approximates the experience of religious awe or, worse, stands in its place. Heschel's critique of this shortfall echoes the teachings of the classical rabbis in Genesis Rabbah 35:5 in their commentary on the covenant of the rainbow, in which God extended to Noah and to humankind the promise that the world will not be destroyed again. The Torah says that God will make the rainbow out of his clouds on the earth and that both parties, God and the people, can look upon the rainbow and remember the covenant. The rabbis sense the inherent pantheistic pitfall: how quickly will it be until said future generations demand that the symbol itself of God's covenant becomes the stand-in for God or for the covenant? The worship of nature proper—especially those natural phenomena that God uses to convey relationship—is a pathetic and misleading substitute for the real thing.

And here especially our lack of the experience of revelation feels particularly acute and sensitive. Much of what we know as Judaism was developed in a self-consciously postrevelatory time, in response to the acute sense that to live this tradition requires something more than self-evident assumptions. The classical rabbis struggled with what it is to be a pious Jew without the affirmation that is mythically imagined to have governed the life of the Israelites at the foot of Sinai, and traveling through the desert, and even in the Holy Temple in Jerusalem. The Bible takes revelation for granted; postbiblical Judaism must construct a system that tolerates the absence of revelation. To do so, the rabbis would have to develop ideologies specifically about certain kinds of seeing, such as their basic distrust of eyewitness testimony, especially in capital cases that have absolute—read: divine—consequences. Much of the organizing systems that rule traditional Jewish life—such as the self-enclosed world of Jewish law—coexist very easily with modernity since they have been so radically severed from revelation or have figured out ways to absorb revelation. But push a bit past the ethnic particularism, beyond the surface commitment to the proper performance of ritual and practice, and there is a core unresolved concern for the absence of a convincing sense of the absolute. Only in reference to the mythic world of Indiana Jones can we relate to God's cautioning to Moses as he pleads to *see* God's *kavod*, God's honor, and believe that humankind cannot see God and actually survive the encounter. If anything, we tend to believe that what we see we know we can subdue.

Modern Jews, I think, are perhaps unconsciously aware of this problem, and have developed a few interpretive strategies to deal with how our sight has affected our psyche. One strategy, still very much in vogue in some communities, is to look away. This is the core stance of Jewish fundamentalism, which embodies somewhat ironically the awareness that looking too closely is dangerous *because there is actually what to see.* The response—intellectually and culturally—is to not look. This too has its roots in classical Jewish thought, especially in the warnings in rabbinic tradition against studying "Greek wisdom." Greekness, or Hellenism, is a stand-in for anything cultural or intellectual that we can make "other" as foreign or polluting. Obeying this dictate literally creates communities that carefully prescribe what kinds of cultural or intellectual influences are allowed to penetrate their boundaries. One school of thought among contemporary Jews argues that the best protection against antirevelatory, antitraditional influences is carefully constructed filters.

A second option is a mystical strategy. Mysticism aspires to true communion with the divine, independent of the sensory experience of the mediated divine. In other words, what we see before us— what appears intelligible—may indeed be obscuring the true meaning that cannot be captured rightly in words or in our mortal vision. Visual clarity and acuity on their own are misleading, almost idolatrous: they make us think that we understand what it is we see. The mystic can survive an encounter with a problematic visual by taking the underlying position of not trusting the folly of his eyesight. This option actually reverses the problem of not having revelation by reveling in its overt absence: life's quest is to seek out the secretive, since the plain meaning of things cannot have absolute meaning anymore.

Related to this approach and also inherent in rabbinic tradition and its responses to its evolving world is the solution to forgo vision in favor of the other senses. The hallmark of rabbinic tradition was its orality, the transmission of ideas and traditions from teacher to student. Like the ancient Greeks, the rabbis believed that losing one's eyesight could actually make someone a "seer"—unencumbered by the visible world, a seer could perceive the truth of the matter. This echoes the modern scientific suggestion that the alternate sensory acuities of the blind are much stronger than they are for the seeing. Blindness in the rabbinic world was not an encumbrance in the passing down orally of ideas; it may have even generated clarity of vision.

But a third approach—since I am not a mystic, since I trust my eyesight, and since our culture has reprioritized the importance of seeing as seeking—is the much more difficult position that we are actually seeing things right, and still enjoined to behold with awe; that awe, inasmuch as it has something to do with seeing, has something more to do with a kind of beholding, something that goes beyond a reflex and to the heart of what it means to create meaning in Jewish life.

This difficult approach is best embodied in a cryptic rabbinic text, a mishnah in Tractate *Hagigah* that speaks specifically to the dangers and opportunities involved with real looking and seeing. It is a text that appears to be far ahead of its time; or perhaps, again, we are reminded that the challenges wrought by emancipation and enlightenment are really not all that new.

The text reads as follows:

> One may not expound the [laws of] forbidden nakednesses in [a group of] three, nor the account of the Creation in two, nor the Chariot alone; unless he was wise and understanding on his own.
>
> Anyone who looks at four things—is deserving to not have come into the world—what is above, what is below, what is before, and what is after. And anyone who does not take compassion on the honor of his maker—is deserving to not have come into the world.

This cryptic mishnah is regulating the study of texts that the rabbis consider to be problematic and suggestive—the first chapters of Genesis, the laws of sexual morality, and the account in Ezekiel in which God is anthropomorphically represented as a majestic chariot departing Jerusalem. In the first portion of the mishnah, the rabbis prescribe the proper number of students who may study these traditions together; in so doing they structure the learning experience to minimize the alienation, loneliness, promiscuity, and confusion that might emerge from improperly accessing this material. In the process, of course, the rabbis also open a window to their own attraction to the material. These prescriptions and guidelines make the promise of what these texts secretly have to offer as tempting as the pomegranate in the Garden of Eden—for there too, the fruit had more to offer than merely the satisfaction of appetite. Not surprisingly, the Talmudic text that follows this mishnah is dominated by discussion, implicitly, of the first two "coping strategies" that I mentioned earlier: the danger of looking at difficult things and when to look away, and the mystical approach to finding secret meanings.

But let us turn back to our mishnah. The mishnah then concludes with its two extraordinary warnings: where not to look—above, below, in front, behind—and the obligation to express compassion at what is ultimately seen. The first warning of the mishnah echoes and reinforces the previous rules provided by the mishnah and adds another layer of seduction to what lies within. These must really be no ordinary texts! Hic sunt leones! The Mishnah does not spell out for us what is to be found above and below, in front or behind, but we might guess: are we talking about where we come from and where we are going, root causes and destinies, heaven and hell, what preceded God chronologically or spatially, what the heavenly realms look like—all the kinds of questions that have no satisfying answers and might well produce the outcome that the Mishnah's fear suggests, a deep existential regret about one's place in the world, even a willingness to accept the curse of preferring not only not to have asked these questions, not to have looked down spooky corridors, but not to have been placed in those corridors to begin with. For some, we suspect this warning might be enough, but I don't think the Mishnah is so naive as to suspect that most readers heed this warning by staying away. By first defining the problematic territory, and then giving warnings about where to wander within, the Mishnah essentially says to us, "Don't go out in the rain! But if you do, take a raincoat."

Of course, this fear of exploration may arise not from what is to be found but rather from the absence of anything to see in this postrevelatory world—from our fear that deep existential and theological explorations will uncover darkness and silence, welter and waste. Perhaps this is what lies in Hayim Nachman Bialik's rendering of this mishnah into a children's song, wherein the answer to the questions "What is up? What is down?" is merely "you and me," hovering on a seesaw between heaven and earth. Is this a critique of the question? Or an expression of despair about the answer?

Or, perhaps, this mishnah is warning about the type of looking. The word here in Hebrew is not *ra'ah*—to see—but *mistakel*—to look, or to glance. Looking can be seeing, in which case it is relational; but looking can also be observing or, worse, voyeuring—which is one-directional and one-dimensional. Perhaps this text is not concerned about what happens when one really engages with what comes before or what is readily unseen but rather with what happens when we merely glance furtively and do not fully see, when we glimpse something that ultimately causes us regret because we do not fully understand it. Indeed, the medieval commentator Nahmanides cites this warning in remarking on the very rainbow of the covenant that we discussed earlier, as part of the fear of what an ignorant or insufficient glance can produce—as opposed to the sustained, meditative looking that tolerates ambiguity as it seeks understanding.

But the second warning in the Mishnah, the last comment, is even more extraordinary. We are no longer in the realm of specific cautions that might pertain to how one studies Torah; we have now journeyed, implicitly as the result of that Torah study, to a place of encounter with the divine or the mysterious, and our behavior in that moment is subject to evaluation. In the moment of the divine encounter, we are told how to behave. We are directed to act compassionately—to exercise compassion for the *kavod*, for the honor, of our maker. We are not told to grovel, to be fearful, to shield our eyes, to avoid the encounter with the divine, to distrust what we see, but rather to be compassionate and respectful in this moment of bold encounter. In other words, our explorations and our knowledge lead us to stand face to face with truth and the divine. And we are judged not on the basis of that accomplishment but on how we act as a result of that encounter. Consider the revelatory moment of an erotic encounter, the experience of suddenly seeing the coveted *other* naked. There is tremendous power in that moment: the seer has the profound capacity for judgment and evaluation, and a failure to act with compassion and love is devastating. It is literally the difference between whether we make the other feel naked and vulnerable, or embraced and cherished.

Of course, this text must also be alluding midrashically to Moses' dialogue with God. Remember that in the book of Exodus, Moses had asked precisely to see this *kavod*, this honor or presence, in order to fully understand his purpose; and he was not allowed. Now, in the postrevelatory age, the rabbis allow for the possibility that our eyes will encounter that very *kavod*—and that that seeing continues to be a tremendous act of power and control that must be closely legislated. In this world of radical possibility, the valuable has become vulnerable.

In the Talmudic discussion that expounds on this last warning, which we will examine further in the epilogue to this book, the rabbis tell of one person who pushed and penetrated his way toward ultimate understanding—Rabbi Akiva, remembered as perhaps the greatest of the sages. As Rabbi Akiva gets closer and closer to the divine retinue, the ministering angels attempt to deflect his advances, but God calls them off, saying, "Leave him be—he is deserving to make use of my honor"—*raui hu l'hishtamesh b'kvodi*, channeling the very language of the Mishnah's warning. In the rabbinic cosmology, humans are vastly superior to the angels who accompany the divine retinue; angels are mere vessels of the divine will, whereas humans are independent reflections of it. We humans may be fallible in our use or misuse of our godliness, capable of choosing evil as readily as we choose good; but the angels, immobile and single-minded, are incapable of defeating the greatest humans when in their quest for the divine these humans reach the highest limits. By telling this story in commenting on the Mishnah, the rabbis highlight what that act of compassion in the moment of revelation must look like. Akiva is celebrated not for the milestone of having journeyed to the heart of truth but for the bravery and willingness in that moment to stand in compassionate awe.

Ultimately, awe is not an intrinsic reality, an instinctive response, or a metaphysical experience. Awe is a *stance*, a voluntary decision to act with compassion upon seeing exposed that which we cherish and value. This is why awe of the heavenly realms—*yir'at shamayim*—is the one behavior that heaven cannot command, why everything is in the hands of heaven except the awe of heaven—precisely because of how far we can reach in our quest for truth, how bold we can become in standing face to face with the divine. The nineteenth century scholar of religion Cornelius Tiele describes the basic human religious impulse as "an original, unconscious, innate sense of infinity"—and I suppose most definitions of awe subscribe to this paradigm. It seems to me that the experience of modernity for Jews has been something of the opposite: it is innately and deliberately conscious. This, then, has generated a conventional course of action, roughly recognizable from Adam in the Garden of Eden and through Kafka and to the present: inquiry, encounter, disappointment, and alienation.

Since we have rejected the paradigm that rejects inquiry and knowledge, our alternative is that we reconstitute a brazen self that digs deep into all there is to know, probes our history and our consciousness, and still decides to both keep looking and to take on a mantle of awe.

I do not mean to suggest that we become blind to the flaws that we see as a result of our inquiring, or that this strange place in which we find ourselves is perfectly comfortable. The notion that we would sweep back the curtain to find less there than we expect, and still manage to compose ourselves and seek an awe-inspiredness, is deeply cognitively and thus emotionally dissonant.

Nor do I mean to confine this entire discussion to the question of faith, and specifically faith in God. In the Jewish experience of modernity, what has been so thrilling and at the same time so challenging has been our penetrating gaze on everything in our tradition that has value—our history, our peoplehood, our traditions, our community. All these are still awe-deserving. When the rabbis talk about *yir'ah* throughout their literature, they tweak the terminology from awe of God—as it is described in the Bible—to awe of the heavens, in their familiar phrase *yir'at shamayim*. The heavens are vast and all-encompassing, they represent actually everything we see. Perhaps the rabbis too were struggling with this very commandment to stand in awe of God, they too living in a world without the obviousness of revelation and its intended effects. This peculiar little mishnah seems to be a window into the consciousness of the rabbis struggling with a familiar problem. The historian Van Harvey, in his book dealing with this same issue and its relationship to Christian faith, says as follows:

> . . . we *cannot* see the world as the first century saw it. We can, it is true, imaginatively understand how they could have believed what they believed, but these beliefs are no longer practically possible for us. We have, as it were, bitten of the apple, and our eyes have been opened and our memories are indelibly stamped with the new vision of reality.

Harvey, following the Christian theologian Rudolf Bultmann, argues that this modern struggle reflects changes in our consciousness that are beyond our control—that the very "furniture of our minds" reflects a kind of knowledge and understanding of the world unknowable and unanticipatable by the authors of our holy texts and the architects of our cherished traditions. To stand in perfect fidelity to those ideas without a consciousness of the leap involved entails either a basic intellectual dishonesty or a reactionary sensibility.

Our awe problem reflects the larger culture of emancipation and enlightenment, where the lack of definitiveness to our Jewishness—to our myths, our history, our traditions, our conviction—inclines us either to slink away from them or to believe we must shut our brains or our souls in order to live with them. I want us to imagine a new reality for Jewish identity—actually, a model that is deeply resonant with much of what rabbinic Judaism is all about—that precariously demands of us two critical imperatives: one, that we live a life of inquiry, eyes wide open, regardless of where it leads and what truths it unmasks; and two, that we maintain a stance of awe, regardless of what our eyes see. More exalted than the experience of awe that comes from seeing awesome things is the possibility of living an awe-inspired life because we choose to do so. This reality has to be what underlies the strange punishment that the Mishnah threatens for those who will not heed its warnings: you will literally regret your life. No one lives in regret because of a major discovery;

we live in regret because we are unable to stand up again and keep looking, with awe, at what we have found.

And again we come back to memory. Some of the preeminent Jewish myths and moments that focus on memory involve the linking of memory and mitzvah through the experience of seeing and/or standing in awe. The treachery of Amalek, which we are commanded to perpetually remember, came about due to a failure of awe: Amalek attacked viciously at a moment of weakness, when Israel was tired, weary, and not *yarei Elohim*—that is, not properly in awe of God. In contrast, during the Seder night, we are commanded to remember the Exodus from Egypt specifically in the obligation *lirot et etzmo ke'ilu hu yatza M'mizrayim*—to see ourselves as though we had just left Egypt behind. And at the heart of the mitzvah of tzitzit, the ritual fringes, is the phrase "And you shall see them, and you shall remember all the commandments of the LORD, and you will perform them." Rather than the sequence of seeing, encountering, and becoming alienated, this is the idealized Jewish sequence—seeing, remembering, and doing. When our eyes are closed, Amalek attacks; when our eyes are open, we are self-conscious, aware of who we are, and purposeful. This means that this awe to which we aspire is more about who we are and what we become, and less about what actually stands before our eyes. Much as selectivity enables memory to be a tool of conscious empowerment, this stance of awe—this act of compassion on our part—makes us ever more aware of who we are and what it is we are encountering.

The best explanation we can provide, then, for this obligation to stand in awe of God, as it is presented in Deuteronomy, is not that God wants the Israelites to hinge their identity on what they saw, once upon a time in a faraway land. It is not that the awe of that moment is supposed to transfer. The attitude instead is this: that we can and will continue to see all sorts of amazing things, and yet the core obligation to be people of awe—something God can never force us to be—will never go away. In fact, that obligation will only grow ever more urgent.

# CHAPTER 3

# Ahavah

## LOVE as DESIRE and PURPOSE

And yet, awe only tells half the story. In classical sources, awe (*yir'ah*) is paired with love (*ahavah*). These two impulses are meant to characterize behavioral stances we take in performance of the commandments—so we do commandments motivated by love and awe—and also serve as independent, supererogatory obligations in their own right. For all the merits of *yir'at shamayim*, awe of heaven, and the importance of awe in religious consciousness, awe pales in comparison to this twin elusive commandment to love God. The centrality of the obligation to love is encapsulated in the words of Judaism's most familiar prayer, the *Shema*, taken from Deuteronomy 5: "And you shall love the LORD your God—with all of your heart, with all of your spirit, and with all of your might."

The cultural familiarity of the *Shema* reinforces the significance of this verse for Jewishness, but it should not obscure quite how difficult and complicated its mandate is. What's more, this is not the only "commanded love"—besides God, the Bible commands us to love the stranger, love the neighbor, and in certain texts, to love the world.

In virtually every one of my Jewish educational environments, we spent time on the essential questions concerning this obligation: How is one commanded to love God—or, for that matter, to express *any* emotion toward *anything*? Can God command love of God? Does the outcome of this obligation actually produce emotion and sentiment? Or does the very nature of commandedness undermine the sentimentality that love connotes? What kind of love does this become?

These questions contain two separate but related problems. The first problem stems from the assumption that the emotions of the human heart cannot be so easily manipulated. For while the human heart may be malleable—as elsewhere in Deuteronomy, God first asks the people to "circumcise" their hearts, and then several chapters later offers to do so directly, ostensibly to prepare them emotionally to stand in covenantal relationship—can we force an emotion on ourselves? One might try to like something, and may even perform actions out of devotion or obedience. But given the idiosyncrasies of emotional experience, can one ever be commanded to love?

The inverse of the problem, a second and related concern, goes to the nature of commandedness in creating this obligation. How would one enforce or evaluate an obligation to love, or assess its proper fulfillment? "Who knows what evil lurks in the hearts of men!" Could it be that the essential, formative commandment, expressed in a text that then emerges at the literal and figurative heart of Jewish prayer, involves an unindictable, immeasurable commandment whose proper performance remains locked in the secrecy of the human heart? This question hearkens back to our earlier discussion of commandedness itself, and how obedience interfaces with the voluntary nature of commitment. If a commandment is issued together with a specific threat—as the midrash playfully describes the Sinai theophany, accept this Torah or I will drop the mountain on top of you—then the obedience that emerges can hardly be characterized as voluntary. This in turn makes a commandment associated with an emotion—the obligation to love God—deeply difficult to understand.

These difficult questions, however, may be in and of themselves problematic, as they are rooted in a specific set of assumptions about love, about who it is we love and how we love. Love, *ahavah*, tends to be portrayed in the familial sense, and thus involves the sense of attachment that is required between us and those to whom we are already intrinsically related or connected. If love is essentially a familial act, a tool of emotional attachment, then this commandment is indeed problematic. How can we be commanded to emote in a certain way? How can this love ever be tested or evaluated? Who knows the inner thoughts or feelings of another? What's more, to be commanded to love those to whom we are already intrinsically connected—parents, or God—means that the commandment echoes a sentiment that we are already wired to feel. One of my friends tells of a conversation he had with his rabbi in yeshiva, in which my friend—a struggling teenager—asked the teacher how we knew of the existence of God. Astonished, the rabbi answered that the question itself was similar to asking how he knew of the existence of his father. In both cases, intimacy between the two makes the question moot. The answer was not helpful for my friend at the time, but it remains a telling one: in the world of commandedness and obligation, I suspect that most adherents start with a certain assumption about the relationship they are expected to have and about the love they are supposed to feel. This assumption tells us to be suspicious of how *ahavah* is described, that it will likely describe the mechanics of an existing relationship. An emotion that is commanded needs to be broad enough to entail all aspects of attaining the relationship.

Maimonides' Book of Love—his section on *ahavah*, one of the fourteen pillars of his epic *Mishneh Torah*—does not appear to be about any such love that we recognize, but rather about commandments that implicitly reflect love of the creator. These commandments include prayer, the wearing of tefillin, and the rules concerning the reciting of the *Shema*. Perhaps these commandments reflect the obligation to love God because they involve specific techniques of binding the obligation physically and literally to the adherent—so we recite the obligation to love God in the *Shema*, or we bind its words to our arms in the tefillin or to our houses in our mezuzot. Alternatively, we make sense of it by relying on the problematic assumption about *ahavah* as articulated earlier. If the Torah's commandment to love pertains to a previously established loving relationship, then this commandedness merely becomes translated to the mechanical vehicles in which that love can be expressed. These behaviors and activities reflect not the love of God but the performance or remembrance of a love of God. Put a different way: if husbands and wives have societally mandated obligations to one another—in Jewish tradition, these include shelter, food, and sex—then one might read those obligations as the performance of the loving relationship. But just as one would never substitute these acts of love for the emotion of love, I think we are mistaken in thinking of commanded acts of love for God as a substitute for the empirical experience of loving God.

Simply put, the codification of love in Jewish tradition should not be misread as love itself. The Talmud famously recounts the story of Rabbi Akiva's martyrdom, wherein at the moment that his skin is being flayed he revels—to his students' alarm and amazement—that he finally now understands how to fulfill the obligation to love God. The commandment of the *Shema* ordered the love of God with one's entire heart, might, and spirit—and with this act of self-sacrifice, he now fulfills the ultimate *act* of love. But even here, Akiva's love is performative: he fulfills the commandment of loving God by doing everything in his power to demonstrate this love. This is not the same as love itself.

And in such a scenario, with the underlying loving relationship taken for granted, should a person experience no rupture, no chasm, in his or her loving relationship to God, Torah, and commandment, then the opportunities to encapsulate and enact that love are liberating. With Akiva, melancholy turns to elation with his climactic ability to make manifest a kind of aching. Akiva is freed at the moment of self-sacrifice to understand that his martyrdom has given voice to an otherwise inarticulable love of God, that his martyrdom fulfills his obligation to love God. By becoming codified in individuals' actions that manifest love, love itself becomes mysterious, arbitrary, stimulated by extrinisic or impenetrable interior forces. Love becomes, in essence, consummation—it becomes the active manifestation or representation of a loving relationship.

This move to equate the fulfillment of the relationship with the commanded emotion that governs the relationship characterizes not just halakhic Judaism, as we have seen manifest in Maimonides, but also charismatic Judaism, in the mystical tradition. The mystical tradition is itself performative in how it seeks to express human love for the divine, although its version of that performance is quite different: Joseph Dan shows how it seeks a direct means of communing with the divine, over and against the sensory techniques—be they language, commandment, ritual—of the normative tradition. Since the goal is ultimate unification with the divine, sensory behaviors at best mediate the experience, and at worst idolatrously *replace* the essence of the experience. The mystical tradition looks askance at systems by which we translate either the words of the Torah into their literal meaning or understand the performance of commandments as literal means of carrying out God's will. Instead, the mystic seeks to commune directly with the divine—a process in which the words of the Torah or the commanded behaviors must be marshaled properly without being the actual tools of this communion.

The most extreme articulation of this process is the *Zohar*'s description of Moses actually copulating with the divine during his revelatory experience atop Sinai. This echoes the mystical teachings about human abilities to unite disparate impulses—sexually and by other means—and in so doing to repair a broken and disunited world. As Yehuda Liebes explains, what makes Jewish mysticism unique in this regard is that the ultimate goal of this unification with the divine is not merely the supernal achievement of the believer but ultimately the act of repair that it brings about for the world. Still, even though this act of loving God also entails loving the world, it manifests in the act of communing with God—literally and figuratively—and it is difficult to separate the metaphor from the goal. As such, the mystics too eroticize the divine-human relationship—this time not through the performance of the commandments per se, but through an attempt to achieve a more direct union.

Of course, this kind of mystical thinking describing this explicit love of God in these terms is scandalous, especially in the context of what we think of as pious Jewish thought. The great scholar of Kabbalah Gershom Scholem goes to great lengths in his discussion of the text just cited about Moses and God to isolate it as unusual, and to maintain that it represents a wayward strand in the tradition. Fearing that the *Zohar* is turned to obscenity, Scholem contrasts the text's prevalent sexual imagery—which he argues mostly describes God's union with Godself—with Christian mysticism's "bridal chambers," which he considers more problematic. Meantime, we might also read the writings of Martin Buber—Scholem's interlocutor as co-inheritor of the mystical tradition—as cautioning against an overly literal reading of the erotic language of communion discerned from the mystical literature. Buber's relational theology of I-Thou elevates this notion of *devekut*, of cleaving to God, from the literal to the relational. Strikingly absent from I-Thou is the practical and normative language that would turn this ideology into a set of practices, as we find both with halakhic Judaism and among the Hasidim.

Taken to its fullest extreme, the attempt to bridge the acts we might do to perform our loving relationship to the actual loving relationship itself can become unbelievably coarse. In her poem "Tefillin," the Israeli poet Yona Wallach famously and controversially imagined the wrapping of the phylacteries as performative sexplay. Even on the tenth reading, the poem is astonishing. Now, few who wrap tefillin see their performance of this ritual through the lens of sadomasochism, to be sure; but Wallach's poetry may reflect a wiser reading of the tradition than it is given credit for. If tefillin bind us to the creator in manifesting an act of love between us and God—if the mitzvah is, in and of itself, the love of God— then the equation to human sexuality, which also manifests (ideally) a loving relationship, is not far off.

So this move by classical Jewish tradition—to describe love through its fulfillment or performance—is totally understandable, but still difficult. It reflects the human need for codification, even when it comes to relationships. We can make a love sacred with proper ceremonies and blessing and by building around it the covenantal infrastructure to enable it to succeed, through commitments and obligation. It is easy to understand how someone who loves God, and loves loving God, wraps tefillin to make manifest that love; it is less obvious how wrapping tefillin makes for loving God, or how one is supposed to read Maimonides or the Kabbalah as a manual for an encounter with an obscure and distant divine. These latter concepts are especially difficult given the rupture of modernity that lies at the core of this book, the conviction that Jewishness can no longer be sustained on the basis of a series of self-evident suspicions and assumptions, on the basis of a visceral experience of the world. If we are to resuscitate a meaningful commandedness, and to experience and perform acts of love as an essential and defining component of that commandedness, we must make that love articulate and transmissible.

We need to be able to describe this ethic of *ahavah*, this commanded love, which the sources assume to be so essential to Jewishness, in language that makes room for a different set of underlying assumptions about the relationship it is meant to describe. What does the obligation look like for someone who is tentative about a relationship rather than someone who is already betrothed? In what ways does this deep loving form a part of a Jewish consciousness and Jewish identity for the skeptical, for the distant—or even for those burned by love?

And in establishing this description, we must also find a way to approach love with the same criteria and pitfalls that applied to our discussion of awe—as a stance that implicates us, that defines what we are more than merely defining the object of the emotion. In this way, we create a principled self-definition in a world at a loss for defined criteria of meaning.

## Babylonian Talmud Tractate *Ketubot* 61b

Rabbi Rehume was a disciple of Rava's in Mehoza. He would regularly visit his wife every year on the Eve of Yom Kippur. One day his studies absorbed him. His wife was waiting for him. "Now he will come. Now he will come." He did not come. She became upset, and a tear fell from her eye. He was sitting on the roof. The roof collapsed under him and he died.

This is a sad parable. Rabbi Rehume—in Aramaic, literally, Rabbi Love—lived apart from his family in order to pursue his true love: a life of Torah study in the schoolhouse of Rava. His wife lived for his annual return, and his failure to return literally kills him. Her heartbreak, encompassed in a single moment of revelatory realization that he is not coming, wreaks a miraculous death and the stark closure to their love story.

This is indeed a story about love and its dangers, but which kind of love? The Talmudic context in which this narrative appears is an extended discussion of the ethics of sexual behavior, and specifically the ramifications of living apart from one's spouse—whether in the service of Torah or for any other profession. This particular story reflects deep ambivalence about this practice, as it responds negatively to a mainstream practice among rabbis and students with the rise of the Babylonian study houses in late antiquity. Clearly the author of this story is displeased with this kind of asceticism and its implicit choices.

But there is also a different message in this story, a tragic love story, rooted in the complexity of commitment and forgetfulness. It seems that this rabbi's forgetfulness is what actually kills him, as his failure to consummate his love for his wife in favor of Torah, the other woman, convinces his wife that he is not coming back. Hope turns to despair, and her conviction moves from suspicion to reality. Rehume is pulled between the love of Torah and the love of his wife; or perhaps between a love of Torah, manifest in his total absorption, and the love of relationship, which would be defined by his ability to remember his commitments. The two visions of love are in essence opposites, the former expressed in total communion with the other and the latter expressed in the craving of the fundamentally unattainable. This latter love fails tragically precisely because of the act of forgetting; the absence of memory causes its undoing. This text describes a basic truth about faith, belief, and their commitments. When we believe in what we do not know, the belief holds up—even if the unknown is distant from us, totally incomprehensible, and sustained only by the conviction of our hearts. When we disbelieve, that otherness fails and dies. If you will it—even if it is actually a dream—it transforms to simply as-yet-unfulfilled reality. And so the moment Rehume's wife no longer believes that her husband will return, he becomes literally unable to return to her.

That this is a love story between Rehume and his wife—even a tragic one—is very telling, given how central the non- or anticonsummation theme is expressed by locating the drama on Yom Kippur. On Yom Kippur, husbands and wives refrain from sexual contact, and this is the one day these two spend together. Their love strangely sustains the two of them alive and in relationship with each other despite this key particularity. Why does the author make the story so odd and antierotic? I think it must be to emphasize that this love is not—or, at least, is more than—simply an erotic relationship. The relationship between Rehume and his wife, flawed as it is, is embodied in its relationality—in the seeking that exists between the two of them. In this way, Rehume's love for Torah—so all-consuming, so dominating of his mind that he cannot remember his humanity, that he becomes precisely unloving—is mocked in comparison to his wife's all-too-human, desperate, seeking love of him. After all, it is her love that ultimately kills him, and no love of Torah can save him.

The Greek philosophical tradition contained a hierarchy of loves, encapsulated in several different words—*filia, eros, agape*—that express aspects of what we call love. The highest level, as articulated in Plato's *Symposium*, is the love that goes beyond friendship and is manifest in *the desire for that which one has not*, and that in turn aspires toward the good and the virtuous. This love is not about satisfying one's appetites, but rather is embodied in the seeking for the goodly other. Here too love is not defined in its fulfillment but in the seeking itself: to love the good is to aspire for it.

In Genesis 8:21, after the flood, God is comforted by the smell of savory sacrifice, and as a result announces that humanity's irrepressible need for sin—"for the inclination of the heart of mankind is evil from its youth"—will prevent it from again being obliterated by flood or otherwise. Rather than lamenting this sorry state of human existence and the dominant ethic of evil, as many commentators do, the medieval commentator Rabbi David Kimchi (known as RaDaK) offers a novel reading of the verse: the appetitive evil inclination precedes the ethical good inclination. Rather than despair of the absence of good, this should make us crave for the good when it is absent. The evil inclination of the heart of mankind should generate a seeking for the good. This is why, according to RaDaK, the subsequent verse in Genesis lists the parallel polarities—heaven and earth, warmth and cold—which keep and reflect the world order; for, after all, it is in relationship and response to evil that goodness acquires its virtue. An evil inclination from a young age is the ground from which the good inclination—the seeking of the good—grows and flowers. In this way, RaDaK's interpretation is profoundly liberating in reversing the pessimistic straightforward reading of the biblical text: goodness becomes that which we aspire to, in spite of—or perhaps because of—our foregoing evil inclination.

To love good—or, in the Bible's language, to love God—is to aspire for God. If our understanding of yir'ah ironically pivots on our sense of power and thus our willingness to hesitate in our judgments, in our understanding of the world, ahavah in turn underscores our basic vulnerability, that which we lack, that then inclines us to reach for the good. When the rabbis turn ahavah into purposefulness, encompassed in the fulfillment of specific obligations, they manifest this understanding of ahavah. But the rabbis' interpretation should not be read to mean that performing those mitzvot is love itself, in an idolatrous way that fetishizes behavior and turns love into something performative. The commandments must be about seeking— not about what has already been found.

The Bible's greatest love story, the Song of Songs, models this love relationship as well. The story in the book describes the pain and longing in the quest of two lovers to find each other in the same place at the same time. One interpretive approach to this description of a love affair is to start from the assumption that there is something deeply problematic about this failure to consummate, and about the text's insistence on focusing on the quest rather than the discovery. This underlies Rabbi Joseph Soloveitchik's famous and defining metaphorical rendering of the story as telling of modern Jewry's need to mind the twentieth century call of history in the founding of the state of Israel. In Soloveitchik's essay "Kol Dodi Dofek"—"The Voice of My Beloved Knocketh"—the knocking of the beloved on the door, God's intervention in history, must be acknowledged by our rousing ourselves from our sleep and opening up the door. This radical theological statement about the presence of God in history, or at least about our responsibility of being *aware* of God's presence in history, demands the fundamental underlying assumption that the unconsummated ending of the Song of Songs betrays a problem with the text; that redemption or restoration involves fixing the story and repairing the outcome. *Unlike* in the Song of Songs, we must get up and answer the door.

Is this necessarily so? What if the Song of Songs is describing the fullness of love as encapsulated in the very seeking itself? In this model, love is not found in the repair of the problem, in the moment at which the two star-crossed lovers embrace at last, but in the knocking on one side and subsequent disappointment, and then the craving and seeking on the other. Perhaps the lack of resolution of which the story tells is intentional: the love that the song celebrates is the love of craving, of seeking, of space and distance.

Ironically, Soloveitchik's stance here is decidedly historical. If one starts from the assumption that the Bible tells part of our story but that its fulfillment lies in our own time, one is then required to believe that that first part of the story is left behind in the past; that we are correcting its failures as much as fulfilling its destiny. This is the case most clearly at the end of Deuteronomy, which leaves Israel perched on the precipice rather than entering the land. What follows in the books of prophets, Judges, and Kings constitutes a series of disappointments and failures. But this should not make us believe that the Torah is therefore an unfulfilled story and a paradigm that needs to be corrected. By telling the story in this way, and ending it before the entry to the land, the Bible becomes aspirational—it lays out a vision for future human participation in the story itself. A consciousness of memory tells us to root our story in the Torah's story, to experience its events and narrations as not merely momentarily or historically significant but as continually significant. We are meant to relive the giving of the Torah, not to count our years from it. Here too, to be in loving relationship to God might require aspiring for the lusting and craving imagined in the Song of Songs—rather than the climax of the *Zohar*.

Similarly, the rabbis like to think about the covenantal experience at Sinai as the huppah, the moment of betrothal between God and the people of Israel. This is the "hook" onto which they can attach the fantasy of the erotic encounter between Moses and the divine, the underlying notion that from a literary standpoint this is a highly erotic moment: the men separate from their wives, purify themselves for several days, and they are greeted both with fireworks and with a contractual document. Frozen in time, the betrothal of the people of Israel with God makes everything that comes later—all the disappointments, heartbreaks, betrayals—into failures. This attitude does characterize later prophetic writers, calling to mind the accusations of "whoredom" that dominate the early chapters of Hosea. But then Hosea writes in 2:19 of the reconnection, the reestablished relationship, with words immortalized in Jewish practice as recited during the wrapping of the tefillin—words of the eternal and ongoing betrothal.

When we live in Jewish history, and not outside of it, we come to see that our past is not a set of experiences that we need to correct or continue but rather a template or a framework in which we hope to live. Love is the overarching principle that defines Jewish purposefulness and that motivates us to seek. Like awe, love is a stance that we take toward our behaviors in the world that, in turn, defines us; together with awe, love reflects one of the key impulses that defines what it means to be Jewish. We fulfill our commandedness through expressions of awe and love.

To be sure, there are pieces of this ideology that bother me even as I write, and that surely will not resonate with readers. I am proposing here that we separate out what we can know about the obligation to love from the object of that love. But if the original commandment is to love God, this is hard to do; and for those for whom faith is lacking or wanting, a framework that stems from loving God feels inaccessible and alienating. This is true for me as well. I hope this revelation about my own struggling with faith is something in which the reader will take comfort. In fact, my attempt to reframe these key terms for a contemporary Jewishness connect to my own very personal sense that while these terms of responsibility are deeply defining to Jewishness, they are at the same time overly rooted in inaccessible definitions. It is hard for me to believe that at the core of Jewishness is either a leap of faith or a suspension of disbelief. I respect people of innate faith, although I sometimes feel as though they are lucky rather than necessarily smart, and that for some reason we have overvalorized faith as a metric of merit rather than as the work of a lifetime journey. In this respect I take the words of theologian Eliezer Berkovits crudely out of context when he discusses faith after the Holocaust:

> In the presence of the holy faith of the crematoria, the ready faith of those who were not there is vulgarity. But the disbelief of the sophisticated intellectual in the midst of an affluent society—in the light of the holy disbelief of the crematoria—is obscenity.

For Berkovits, the complexity of the modern Jewish condition with respect to faith requires a stance difficult to maintain—as he says, "This is not a comfortable situation; but it is our condition in this era after the Holocaust." Ultimately, "if there be no breakthrough, the honest thing is to remain at the threshold." This condition of the struggle of faith cannot and should not remain in the provenance only of those who suffered in the Holocaust or experienced its immediate aftermath; the Holocaust may be the contemporary context in which the challenge of theodicy played out in its most graphic and grotesque ways, but the problem is not new. Still, Berkovits gives us language that liberates us from faith as a litmus test for meaningful Jewishness, forcing the legitimacy of skepticism on the believer and the responsibility to respect belief and the unknown on the agnostic.

I also understand and respect those Jews who go the mystical or spiritual route, who cognitively may not believe in objective divine truths as traditionally mandated, but seek other approaches to truth and consciousness. I respect the humility of the process of acknowledging that our rational minds do not know all there is to know in the world. But I am not sure that the only stable options for salvaging the Jewish life of the skeptical Jew are luck, mysticism, or spirituality. Is it possible for us to make these categories continually accessible to a Jewishness that is uninspired by them?

A second personal confession: I am frequently asked, as a historian of ancient Judaism, how it is that I reconcile my lived Jewishness with the knowledge of the fabrication of pieces of Jewish myth and memory. In other words—if you know that there are historical or sociological causes and effects underlying the formulation of Jewish behaviors, what would motivate you to continue to live by those rules? I find these questions curious, and I look to my own motivations as a historian: why would I study something I hated or wanted to destroy? Though there are definitely some scholars in Jewish studies who seek to debunk, demystify and thus to devalue, sometimes in the interest of propping up an alternative narrative and sometimes in acting out a kind of rebellious instinct, most scholars are in this business to spend their lives seeking to know more about things they care about. I may be a skeptic about the historical origins of rabbinic Judaism, but I study it because I care about it even in its denuded form.

Here, though, the same pressing problem lies: why do we assume that knowledge of our past and an intimate relationship to its truth necessarily create distance from that past and a lack of fidelity to it? Are fidelity and passion encompassed only in secrecy and hiddenness, in not knowing or in distant relationship? Do we love less those to whom we are most close? To be sure, there is eroticism in the hidden, which is why the Torah refers to forbidden liaisons as "the uncovering of nakednesses" and why the first moments of awareness in the Garden of Eden are greeted with fig leaves. Some of the seduction of relationship can be found in the mystique that we foster and generate. But that is not to say that one who is exposed is unloved, or that love and passion disappear in moments of revelation. If my scholarship uncovers questions about authenticity or originality, then the text or story before me has become vulnerable. It does not make for an immediate departure of either awe or love; but it does place a greater burden on me to make a case for both.

For *ahavah* to be a defining characteristic of contemporary Jewishness, it should mean purposefulness—the pursuit of the good and ethical stemming from an underlying sense of obligation, and from a sense of what our basic individualism left alone will necessarily lack, as well as in dialogue with the stance of *yir'ah* that we understood earlier. Awe and love become the complementary entities that they need to be—one entailing a heavy pause in the moment of judgment, the other the move forward despite anxiety and uncertainty. My teacher Rabbi Sharon Cohen Anisfeld shared with me her understanding of the biblical category of *gilui arayot*, the forbidden sexual relationships grouped together under the puzzling terminology "uncovering (illicit) nakednesses." Rabbi Anisfeld suggests that we understand this term literally in building a new Jewish sexual ethic: we are forbidden to allow or make our lovers feel the shame of nakedness—even when they are unclothed. I am suggesting we move from this case study to a broader application of this normative terminology.

This framework does not make love any easier. As straightforwardly as the commandments to love God and neighbor are put forth, they are still difficult to achieve. And of course this becomes even more difficult when we move away from the tools of fulfillment of that commandment and toward a more challenging "stance." There are two rabbinic teachings that take the Golden Rule and describe it as defining the entirety of the Torah. In one, Rabbi Akiva says that "Love thy neighbor as thyself" is a "great principle of Torah." In the other, in what seems like a critique of the parallel story in the New Testament, Hillel says that the reverse teaching—that which is hateful to you, do not do to others—defines the entirety of the Torah, with one small addendum: "Now go and learn." In other words, and in stark contrast to Jesus' use of the same teaching as a core defining principle, this version of love made into action is merely a sufficient impetus for one to then go and acquire Torah. It is not that loving one's neighbor achieves all of Torah or is an adequate substitute; rather, it is a trigger behavior that creates the impetus to generate a life of purposefulness in fulfillment of the Torah's mandates.

The relationship of love to Torah does more, however. Just as we saw how awe was linked to seeing and comprehending, so too we see now that love is connected to learning as a form of seeking. This message is encapsulated in the liturgy that the rabbis craft around the *Shema* prayer—from the creation of the firmaments and light, to the revelation of Torah as an act of love, and through the *Shema* itself and onto the redemption that is addressed afterward. The liturgy begs—"Merciful father, merciful one—have mercy on us" and grant us the capacity to understand and become enlightened, to hear, learn, and teach. Mercy and love, learning and seeking are intertwined as mirroring acts of one another.

And when we go back to our opening question, to the centrality of the *Shema* and the obligation to love: perhaps some of its significance stems from the place of the commandment in the narration of the book of Deuteronomy, as part of the very act of selective retelling of the covenantal narrative. Love lies at the intersection of the story we are telling and our seeking to be a part of that story. The obligation to love means that we aspire to covenantally fulfill our obligations and responsibilities, as encapsulated or expressed in the narration of the mythical past.

At the same time, the attribute of love also characterizes and must govern how we embrace our world. In the previous chapter I discussed a new model for thinking about "awe"—that rather than simply representing the act of being passively arrested and frozen by what we see before us, we can achieve a sense of deep awe even in the intensity of what we see. But inasmuch as *yir'ah* and *ahavah* inevitably travel together, the second step is the loving hermeneutic that comes next—the willingness to read charitably, to love despite flaws, and, more important, to be moved and taken in by those things that have already shown us their vulnerability. Our past and our texts are deeply flawed. All scholars know this. For some scholars, wisdom lies in using their knowledge to deflect the flaws, to mask them in the face of the general public, to leverage knowledge for power. But the eternal truth-claims of a text and its ability to inspire us have little to do with accuracy or perfection, much as none of us in our personal lives love perfect people. It comes in our charitable willingness to read a text and relate to it with love.

In an extraordinarily graphic textual moment that has been liturgized both into the circumcision rite as well as into the Passover Seder, the prophet Ezekiel (16:1) describes the union of the people of Israel with God using a metaphor of two lovers in a deeply imbalanced relationship:

The word of the LORD came to me: Mortal, make known to Jerusalem her abominations, and say, Thus says the LORD God to Jerusalem: Your origin and your birth were in the land of the Canaanites; your father was an Amorite, and your mother a Hittite. As for your birth, on the day you were born your navel cord was not cut, nor were you washed with water to cleanse you, nor rubbed with salt, nor wrapped in cloths. No eye pitied you, to do any of these things for you out of compassion for you; but you were thrown out in the open field, for you were abhorred on the day you were born. I passed by you, and saw you flailing about in your blood. As you lay in your blood, I said to you, "Live! and grow up like a plant of the field." You grew up and became tall and arrived at full womanhood; your breasts were formed, and your hair had grown; yet you were naked and bare. I passed by you again and looked on you; you were at the age for love. I spread the edge of my cloak over you, and covered your nakedness: I pledged myself to you and entered into a covenant with you, says the LORD God, and you became mine. Then I bathed you with water and washed off the blood from you, and anointed you with oil. I clothed you with embroidered cloth and with sandals of fine leather; I bound you in fine linen and covered you with rich fabric. I adorned you with ornaments: I put bracelets on your arms, a chain on your neck, a ring on your nose, earrings in your ears, and a beautiful crown upon your head. You were adorned with gold and silver, while your clothing was of fine linen, rich fabric, and embroidered cloth. You had choice flour and honey and oil for food. You grew exceedingly beautiful, fit to be a queen.

God *sees* the people for who they are—despised, discarded, degraded, disregarded. Israel is a child wallowing in the blood of childbirth, a blood metaphor that also anticipates the erotic encounter that follows. The seeing, the compassion, and ultimately the love are all linked—and all precede the cleansing that concludes and climaxes the paragraph. It is we who bring holiness to the texts that we read and sanctity to our lives' purposes, we who give dominion to God and who repair the world. All of these are acts of love—not the love intrinsic and flowing in our blood, but a generative love that derives from our seeing precisely what is lying vulnerable before us.

This is the difference between a life lived passively, which many tend to identify as the core of religious experience—awe toward what is awe-inspiring and the love that follows—and a life lived actively, in which acts of awe and love are undertakings to which we commit.

Indeed, the Mekhilta—an early rabbinic commentary on Exodus—illuminates precisely how these verses found a place at both the Passover Seder and the circumcision rite. The rabbis read Israel's nakedness and vulnerability as an indication that they were without merit when God came upon them. But rather than making the divine-human relationship entirely dependent on God's compassion for Israel, a view of grace that would resonate much closer to Luther than to classical Judaism, God gave Israel two blood commandments that would justify divine intervention: the covenantal blood of circumcision and the relational blood of the Passover sacrifice. "By your blood"—by the blood of these acts of love—you shall "live" into covenantal relationship with the divine. The Jewish historical narrative, in this characterization, relies on two profound acts of stepping forward at moments of extraordinary vulnerability. We circumcise infants right after their arrival in our arms; the Israelites made the Paschal offering *before* the redemption in the hope that their leap forward would be rewarded. Love represents the ability to step forward into relationship without knowing the outcome.

Easier said than done. In one of their many discussions of the ways in which yir'ah and ahavah conflict or hang in the balance, the rabbis discuss who might be able to perform these acts of both love and awe simultaneously, how they might be embodied together. This would be an extraordinary accomplishment, for as we have seen this is equivalent to stopping and starting at the same time, to the mutually essential stances for Jewish modernity of hesitation and action, of mediated comprehension and unmediated purposefulness. The rabbis conclude that only God can achieve these attributes simultaneously, but here the rabbis use a different name for God—Makom, or "the place." The rabbis play with the words, since ba-Makom can mean both "in God" and "instead of." One cannot find love in the place of awe, or awe in the place of love; the two can only be found together in "the place," in God-as-place. This suggestive divine name connotes perhaps the absence of what fills the place that God occupies. The rabbis here deeply understand and reject the instinct to use these verbs of love and awe to condition one another, and understand their necessity to the human condition as vehicles of lived religious experience—even as they can conflict. If *ahavah* is to govern our feet in dictating purposeful action, those feet must have a place to stand; and as we seek that place—divinity, restoration—we must be prepared to both love and stand in awe.

# CHAPTER 4

# Hurban

## CATACLYSM and CREATIVITY

> It is a paradox of events such as the Holocaust that they tend to invite myth-making. One would imagine that the horrors of reality would be sufficient.
> —Ruth Franklin, "How Do We Understand the Holocaust?"

> We cannot retreat to the luxury of being overwhelmed.
> —Ruth Messinger

It would be impossible to write a book about Jewish memory in the shadow of the twentieth century and not devote special attention to the memory of the Holocaust, just as it would be remiss to take stock of the history of Jewish memory and not consider the central place of *hurban*—destruction—as a major catalyst and site of how Jews thought about the past and worked to transcend it.

We have hovered at various times around a discussion of how the destruction of the Temple served as a key rupture in the ancient

Jewish past; and I suggested earlier that the classical rabbis bred a form of "radical continuity" in the face of empirical realities that contested their very actions. This destruction catalyzed the creating of an ideology for how to manage change in times of crisis, related to two discrete concerns: on one hand, the ancient temple constituted the literal and metaphorical central site for Jewish worship and practice. Although the seeds for the reconstitution of Jewish life and practice that would flourish for later Jewish history—synagogue, localized ritual, study and practice, the vitality of "diaspora"—were sown before the destruction of the Temple, the destruction itself required and thus prompted a conceptual restructuring of Jewishness. This is encapsulated powerfully in the narratives that later rabbinic Judaism told about its founding father, Rabbi Yohanan ben Zakkai, symbolically capturing what was actually a radical shift in both elaborate stories and in brief teachings such as this:

> If the holiday of Rosh HaShanah falls out on Shabbat—in the Temple, they would blow shofar, but not in the provinces. When the Temple was destroyed, Rabban Yohanan ben Zakkai decreed that they would blow shofar in any place where there was a court. (Mishnah Rosh Hashana 4:1)

No minor matter this, the establishment of the paradoxical "new precedent." For a culture that prides itself on the importance of tradition and transmission—more on this later—the bold act of decreeing change in response to historical realities bespeaks a conviction of responsiveness to crisis embedded at its heart.

But the rupture was not just specific to Jewish life and practice. A second defining feature lay in the theological implications of this cataclysmic loss. Ritual, narrative, and a framing of memory may work to bridge the threshold between the Jewish past and present when it comes to a rupture of institutional life and how Jewishness is to be practiced; but it does not quite account for how we are to reckon with the grotesque implications of mass death, exile, and slavery, and with the numbness brought about by catastrophic destruction. Fixing the shofar problem may create institutional or even ideological stability, but it does not mend the weariness or brokenness wrought by destruction. And indeed, something is altogether theologically broken in Jewish life in the wake of the past century, which witnessed not just the devastation of European Jewry and the incomprehensible murder of millions of Jews in both systematic and arbitrary ways but also the exiles, persecution, and forced evacuation of Jews from Arab lands and more recently an ambivalent dynamic of power and powerlessness raised in Israel's triumphs and sufferings over the past four decades. No wonder the memory anxiety we discussed earlier! We fear both the consequences of forgetting as well as the consequences of continuing to hold on to these searing images and the memory stain they leave behind.

And here again, there is rabbinic precedent, even as it feels impoverished relative to the complexity of our current condition:

## Tosefta Sotah 15:11–15

> When the Second Temple was destroyed, separatists increased in Israel who would not eat meat or drink wine. Rabbi Joshua set upon them. He said to them, "My children, why do you not eat meat?" They said to him, "How can we eat meat? Every day the daily sacrifice used to be offered upon the altar, and now it is no longer." He said to them, "Why do you not drink wine?" They said to him, "How can we drink wine? Every day it was poured out for libation on the altar, and now it is no longer." He said to them, "Let us not eat even figs and grapes, for they used to bring first-fruits from them on Shavuot. Let us not eat bread, for they used to bring the two loaves and the showbread from them. Let us not drink water, for they used to offer libations from it on Sukkot."
>
> They were silent.
>
> He said to them, "My sons: Not to mourn at all is impossible, for the decree has been declared. But to mourn excessively is also impossible. Rather, thus the sages have said, 'A man shall plaster his home with plaster and leave over a small bit as a remembrance of Jerusalem. A woman may prepare all her ornaments and leave off a little bit as a remembrance of Jerusalem,' as it is said, 'If I forget thee, O Jerusalem, let my right hand forget its cunning; let my tongue cleave to my palate if I

do not remember you, if I do not set Jerusalem above my highest joy.'"
(Ps. 137:5)

All who mourn over Jerusalem will merit to see her joy, as it is said, "Rejoice with Jerusalem and be glad for her, all who love her, join in her jubilation all who mourn over her." (Is. 66:10)

In the wake of the destruction, in the face of a cataclysm that disrupted the natural order of the world, some students responded by deliberately rupturing their own fixed order. Since the systems of Jewish life were tied to the centrality of the Temple, its disappearance generated a dissonance that led the most affected to sever their ties to all Temple-related behavior. Again, Festinger: what happens when prophecy fails?

This behavioral instinct toward paralysis is not specific only to the destruction of the Temple. In modern Jewish theology, this tendency finds an imperfect analogy in the idea that the Holocaust constitutes a permanent rupture in time, sometimes called a caesura, which calls into question the continuity between foretime and aftertime. This is one way to make sense of a broken world: to see in the very conspicuous brokenness a moment that allows for, or even demands, altogether new systems, or at least an abandonment of whatever systems were perpetuated in the old model. It seems to me that part of the instinct in post-Holocaust theology to interpret time in this way—with a rupture at the center—was a means of saving Jewish theology and community, that without this interpretation it would be hard for many to reconstitute a sense of belonging to a continuous timeline of Jewishness. It just all felt too broken—in Arthur Cohen's words, a complete incomprehensible inversion.

But in the process, did this idea about the rupture of the Holocaust unwittingly let the next generation off the hook? In moments of crisis, Jewish thought sometimes invokes a category of teaching called *hora'at sha'ah*—lessons or instructions specific to a moment of urgency that do not become precedent. Urgency creates specific compensatory needs, and the system safeguards against the lasting worth of those panic-induced decisions that may have lacked for sufficient cooking time. Rabbi Jonathan Sacks wisely links this textual exercise to the broader enterprise of creativity and innovation within the world of Jewish law—a body of ideas in which creativity and innovation feature enormously, even as these attributes hide within coded frameworks. Perhaps the idea of caesura is just such a teaching, a mechanism to liberate us from stunned silence in the face of the crises of modern times, be they the general challenges of modernity or the specific horrors of the Holocaust. Yerushalmi too, in other words, is a caesurist—seeing in the breach an impassable chasm to the past that allows for radical new opportunity. And again, Yerushalmi and this kind of post-Holocaust theology leave us in a lurch, as we sense that we must choose between the immediacy of current time and the deeper past to which we feel intrinsically, innately more deeply connected—even across this chasm, across this breach between us and our heritage. The more exciting and difficult challenge is how to take seriously the rupture as having a major effect on our consciousness, while figuring out a way to still live in deep relationship with what precedes it.

In our text, Rabbi Joshua sets upon these students to rebuke them, sensing that their stance would destroy the entirety of the Jewish religious system. Using the logic of reductio ad absurdum, Rabbi Joshua shows the students that in fact the Temple was even more significant than their separatist behavior represented, that it symbolically incorporated every aspect of human life. The failure of the Temple as institution should not thus mean the end of life as we know it, even if the question of how to lead that life—ethically, morally, religiously—was now perilously in question.

Instead, Rabbi Joshua proposes an equally discontinuous solution—the invention of small-scale, symbolic rituals to mark loss, thereby preventing loss from becoming all-defining and all-consuming. The difference in the discontinuity, however, between the proposed solution of the extremists and that of Rabbi Joshua is that his solution externalizes discontinuity and names it in behavioral terms. By doing this act, or by marking this ritual, you are doing something different from what you did before; but you are operating within the same symbolic vocabulary that defined your behavior previously. This approach generates internal continuity through Jewish tradition, rationalizing the discontinuity in the very language of continuity. This is the extraordinary feature of the rabbinic enterprise in general, which made it so successful in adapting to evolving circumstances and so suggestive as a tool for contemporary Jewish renewal: it manages to hybridize rupture and tradition, such that the two neither sever each other nor merely "respond" to each other—they are part and parcel of the same enterprise. Gershom Scholem describes tradition as "the medium through which creative forces express themselves." Innovation is essential to, and not opposite, tradition. This reasoning then helps explain how the scholar and commentator, as the mediators of the productive and creative process, emerge as such significant leaders and social definers in Jewish life. Rabbi Joshua models for us a technique by which we might incorporate the rupture and traverse it.

I like this teaching and the metaphor, but only in theory. The Holocaust and its memory are deafening, and the analogy from the destruction of the Temple breaks down when we think about scale, magnitude, and even the sheer motivation of those who stood against us in this last generation to destroy us. The Romans were many things, but they were not genocidal. Nor did they live just a few years ago. This book is about memory and about the developing of systems that enable us to bridge our past with our present, but I do not want to elide the recent past, to pretend that cultural short-term memory and long-term memory must function in identical ways (even as I hope that the ideology that Jews have developed over a long period of time helps us understand the recent past.)

We still lack the systems as Jews to integrate the Holocaust into our identities in a way that becomes neither reductive nor banal. And as a result, we are anxious. Memory of the Holocaust—or, more specifically, the fear of losing it—is the subject of much Jewish conversation these days. Jews tend to bemoan the loss of memory in the news and editorial pages, and to either celebrate memory or model means of reclaiming it in the arts and culture pages. The lament over memory overlaps confusingly with what seems to be a preponderance of the production of the "stuff" of memory, such that the recording of survivor testimony—ostensibly a response to what was seen as a crisis in impending memory loss—actually reiterates the crisis rather than alleviating it. Perhaps this happens because although codifying a narrative onto film ensures that the story exists, the medium exposes the shallowness of a video testimonial as compared to the experience of hearing a person narrate his or her own experience in person. Few people record their children's first steps merely to seal the experience in time, or to validate its truth for years to come; one hopes in recording such milestones to one day sit with family and watch the film, complementing the preserved testimonial with an ongoing commentary, with an accompanying and evolving "oral tradition." In the U.S. Holocaust Memorial Museum in Washington, the testimonials of survivors are folded into the narration provided by the experience of walking through the exhibits. Their function is not archival but pedagogical. I suspect that although a survivor and his children may sigh with relief as the survivor's Holocaust story is unburdened and stored for posterity, that very storage will inevitably feel hollow when storage is all it is.

Meantime, Jewish anxiety over memory has also spawned its fair share of cultural output—films, stories, books, art—from among not only the survivor generation, and not only the descendants of survivors, but increasingly simply from mainstream creators. Here too this cultural output promotes anxiety rather than putting it to rest, in no small part because the choices involved in each film or book upset other survivors and their descendants, and create a competitive playing field in which a war over right memory is waged. In this climate, the universally agreed upon villains appear to be those whose "memories" are either fabricated wholesale or, more troublingly, partially fabricated—either by survivors who artistically modify their narratives or by artists who use the cultural medium of the Holocaust or the Jewish past to tell a politically or personally significant tale. In James Frey's letter to his readers, written after his memoir of addiction was deemed publicly to be "inaccurate," he acknowledged the complexity of the memoir genre: difficult to subject to journalistic standards, deriving from deeply personal and often unverifiable experience, "about impression and feeling, about individual recollection." Frey's saga finds some parallel in the Jewish community in the sad Binjamin Wilkomirsky tale, in which the author appears to have fictionally crafted a Holocaust memoir. Theories abound as to why someone would do this, ranging from the charitable (he was influenced by the power of suggestion) to the critical (he sought fame and influence.) Interpretations also abound as to the lasting merits of his tale: Does its falsehood make it irrelevant? Or does its power derive less from its historical authenticity and more from his "ferocious vision, a powerful narrative . . . [and] accumulation of indelible images," in the words of one reviewer—features that outlast a factuality debate? In either case, the phenomenon is perplexing. As Thane Rosenbaum writes:

> Holocaust memoirs become so ubiquitous that some people actually pretended to be survivors, absurdly making up stories about concentration camps and crematoria for the purpose of gaining admission to an exclusive club that no sane person would voluntarily wish to join.

Poor memory, in the Jewish imagination, whether willful or accidental, is not just "not memory"; it actually becomes *antimemory*, somehow setting back the memory agenda. The memory of the Holocaust in the popular imagination has followed such circuitous and confusing routes that Rosenbaum continued and asked: "When the gatekeepers and eyewitnesses are gone, will anyone feel guilt about all that amnesia?" Which loss is worse—the loss of the eyewitnesses or the loss of the gatekeepers? The eyewitnesses know the real story; the gatekeepers preserve the production of the right story. In this regard, we know there to be no shortage of cultural productions of the selected Jewish past, from the increasing fiction writing of young Jewish authors to more and more Holocaust films drawing on true-obscure or mythic-real previously unscreened Shoah stories. Outside the newspapers and bookshelves, Jewish memory tends to be architecturalized into buildings and memorials. Inevitably, of course, controversy arises around each particular physical manifestation of specific memorial choices. The past should be codified, rendered into historical narrative, pocked by artifacts . . . is the truth of history rejected or celebrated in artistic representation?

The same sort of concern is periodically raised by critics about formulaic memory, and about the ways in which survivor memorials tend to follow certain literary themes. As we discussed earlier, when memory is rooted in its relationship to reality and evaluated as history, then invalid memory becomes fantasy masquerading as fact. This is the challenge that the *yizker bikher*, the memorial books produced by Jewish survivors in tribute to the towns and villages from which they came, faced in entering the mainstream of Jewish literature. In the 1950s and 1960s, groups of survivors began collecting and recollecting whatever they could about their towns, cities, and communities and poured them out into these volumes. These books constitute a genre only in the most tyrannical sense of the word; though some bear structural or rhetorical similarity to one another, and though we must assume that the publishing houses in Israel (where most were produced) succeeded at stylizing many of the books toward a shared aesthetic, the books are completely idiosyncratic, each an independent artifact. The books feature stories about a town, perhaps a map of a village, a history of the Nazi arrival and decimation, and invariably a list of names: the actual stuff of memorialization encapsulated in the name of the book. There are hundreds of such books, and their obscurity lies in the circumstances surrounding their function: in many cases the books were produced for the annual or regular gatherings of the survivors themselves, almost like a prayer book or ritual manual, a means of codifying or making tactile what they otherwise feared would be subject to the whims and vagaries of their minds.

The books are a thorny problem for historians, and thus are generally ignored, their narratives unverifiable and the methodology completely scattered. It is not surprising, yet deeply sad, that the books were also wildly inaccessible to the survivors' descendants, who often did not read or speak the languages in which they were written, or were not familiar with the shorthand they employ, and the books can be freely found accumulating dust in used bookstores in Israel. Meant both as repositories of narrative and stimulants thereto, the books' absence of a meaningful pedagogy to turn their contents into an intergenerational conversation makes them impenetrable.

The *yizker bikher* represent a threefold tragedy: they tell tragic and unfathomable stories, so tragedy lies in the pages; there is a basic human tragedy in the fear of memory and the inability to transmit the depths of our own experiences that prompts the writing of books like these, the spilling forward of undigested life and death into what ultimately become difficult-to-define mnemonic devices for their bearers; and third and most pathetic, there is tragedy in the total failure of this genre of literature to have a meaningful impact beyond the immediate circles of survivors who wrote the books. Partly because of the costs involved, partly because of what the books were intended to do, the books had extremely limited runs; invariably a next generation of Jews was mystified to find these books on their parents' and grandparents' shelves, and this is why such books can be found principally in those Jerusalem bookshops, as well as in the Library of Congress and various Holocaust museums. Only recently have more than a handful of scholars attempted to make use of the material. A fourth tragedy comes to mind: the violence inflicted on this literature of memory by historians loathe to use such stories because of their failure to employ proper historical methods in telling their stories or preserving their material. One dark feature of Holocaust studies is that the meticulous record keeping of the Germans makes for a much more coherent field of what some skeptics and cynics refer to as "perpetrator studies." It is much more difficult to tell a complete, historically accurate story from the perspective of the survivor. Cue the memory anxiety track.

And then memory anxiety is most complex in cultural realms—art, music, fantasy, fiction—where the relationship between the influence of memory and the category of truth is most fuzzy and problematic. In some cases, this cultural production represents the attempts of a second and third generation to express its own "memory." Psychiatric evidence suggests that children of Holocaust survivors inherit some of the response to trauma from their parents; that while the Holocaust experience itself cannot be transmitted, there is some transmission of how to respond to crisis. It is not clear whether this inherited response is a consequence of mimicking-mirroring, or whether this happens because inevitably Holocaust survivors parent differently. The difference is instructive, as it gets at what it means to transmit this kind of memory. If a child is subconsciously mimicking a response that he sees in a parent, then he is inheriting part of the memory—that is, the consequence of the memory (albeit without the core traumatic experience that generated the response in the parent.) However, if the response to trauma is transmitted to the child through the parenting process—that is, the child is not witnessing and mirroring a behavior but learning or intuiting—then that child's memory is its own first-order memory. If a trauma survivor becomes an abusive parent, for instance, then the child suffering that abuse is experiencing his or her own first-order memory of trauma—in the abuse—even as that abuse might psychiatrically represent a transmission of the different first-order trauma experienced by the parent. When we talk about the transmission of trauma from one generation to the next, we must be mindful of which trauma we are talking about—the one experienced by the original survivor or the one experienced by having lived close to the survivor. And even where we might resist the terminology of inheritance or transmission, in the words of David Harris—a Jewish leader of this "second generation"—this generation bears the enormous weight of "knowledge, emotional freight, and responsibility."

Nevertheless, the rhetoric around the transmission of the Holocaust to second- and now third-generation survivors—the children and grandchildren of Holocaust survivors—adheres to neither of these paradigms, instead revolving around the actual memory itself. According to this conception, in some way one's descendants take ownership, either consciously or subconsciously, of the trauma of the Holocaust itself. This is not the mere ownership or transmission of narrative, a passing-on that does not require familial ancestry; a storyteller can be effective whether or not the story happened to his or her parents or grandparents. Instead, this dynamic tends to take on an existential quality. In these paradigms, a survivor's children, and perhaps grandchildren, inherit almost genetically the survivor experience and thus are enabled to speak as witnesses of a sort. Their testimonial may not directly reflect the lived experience, but it reflects a mediated version thereof. Accordingly, their output is oftentimes mediated output—art, poetry, fiction, and the like (if not memoirs of their own experiences growing up with survivors.)

Naturally, the counter-rhetoric to these kinds of memory claims is equally intense and quite vociferous, as not all survivors—and not all observers, for that matter—are comfortable with the primacy of place taken by the descendants of the survivors in owning the legacy of the Holocaust narrative. Of course, at issue is whether or not these survivors of survivors see themselves as taking something or simply inheriting something. This is the point on which hinge the nasty polemics that are cast back and forth.

Of course, it is easy to see that with the passing of time that very vociferousness about who owns a memory fades for subsequent generations who never bore the weight of the memory itself or its consequences. All the jokes about two Jews on a desert island with their three synagogues—because each must have a synagogue they would not set foot in—are sadly echoed by the realization that it is not merely these internecine conflicts that are lost on the descendants of the custodians of memory, it is also the purported treasure at the memory's heart. This is the humorous but sad motif throughout Aaron Lansky's memoir about saving Yiddish books, as he finds himself despised by but ultimately outliving the competing Yiddish culture organizations that battle each other in increasing folly.

And so amazingly—in the world of survivor testimonials, in the realms of truth and fiction, in the face of extraordinary cultural production, in light of generations rising up to own the memories of their disappearing survivor relatives—the anxiety about the memory of the Holocaust persists. The notion of "Holocaust fatigue"—that in some ways we are overwhelmed by the output about and since the Holocaust—is now thirty years old, having been born well before the outburst of commercial films (fact and fiction) about the Holocaust, the spate of literary creativity, the archiving of testimonials, and the building of buildings. And I wonder whether the problem reflected in this anxiety cannot be reduced to "too much Holocaust," as some critics claim, or "too little Holocaust," as we hear from others. What we have now—it is too much, and it is not enough. The Holocaust has no clearly defined space in our consciousness. Its magnitude demands it be everything, and our human nature and increased distance from the event dictate that it not. So we wrestle with its legacy, conflicted as to what happens when we push back as much as when we let it consume us. In her trenchant essay "How Not to Remember and How Not to Forget," Ruth Wisse indicts the Holocaust Museum in Washington on a manifestation of this exact concern: what is it to be a building preserving the memory of Jewish death while remaining ambivalent about ongoing Jewish concerns? A massive government building, with a $53 million annual budget—and, somehow, still not enough.

Perhaps Ruth Franklin, in her recent book on Holocaust memoir and fiction, gets us part of the way there. Franklin writes: "Every canonical work of Holocaust literature involves some graying of the line between fiction and reality." In making this case, Franklin breaks down the difference between the two genres—not in order to demonize the memoirists but, ironically, in order to redeem them. Artistic expression, to paraphrase Franklin, can articulate a truth of survival and human experience often more effectively than what we allege, impossibly, to be unadorned memory. Not only is there no such thing, but to resist the literary and artistic impulse, whether in reshaping a memory at the core of the literature or in suppressing the creative impulse to say something meaningful and big about the Holocaust, ultimately and paradoxically only grants a privilege of place to bad literature—which might in its poverty come across as more credibly authentic.

And now we find ourselves on uneven ground, as aware as we must be that grappling with the questions of myth, truth, narrativity, and memory with respect to the Holocaust entails asking essential and yet still unasked questions, and that this silence may be part of what makes us mute about making meaning of the Holocaust. We are miles from Rabbi Joshua, even as part of me wants to grasp at a move toward his small-scale ritual, his symbolic markings, as the only technique by which we might both integrate a sense of loss and also move along with our journey.

I wonder aloud then, highly unconfident around issues of this fragility, whether some of our prevailing culture of Holocaust memory, even in its most heroic forms, must belong in the category of hora'at sha'ah that I discussed earlier. The speed with which the deniers of humanity have begun to question the veracity of the Holocaust has forced us into a preposterous defensive posture. The viciousness of the critique has made the historian Deborah Lipstadt into a genuine if unlikely Jewish hero through her willingness to testify over and over again on behalf of those who could not bear

witness themselves. But the consequence of this is that we find ourselves playing the same game as those who would deny the Holocaust, in arguments about facts and accuracy. The reality is even
worse than that: no historical narrative has *ever* withstood the test
of time intact. It is simply impossible to compete with evolving scientific (and pseudoscientific) methodologies that will continue, invariably, to find new ways to question the validity of the foregoing
story. This is the methodological equivalent to the problem of history that I spoke of earlier: it is exceedingly hard not to look down
at a past that we look back on. If Holocaust denial is this bad now,
in the face of living survivors, will it not get inevitably worse? And if
this happens, are we not left waiting, like the hapless Israelites in
the Book of Judges, for another heroic redeemer to come along and
rescue us from our travails?

Franklin provides a partial antidote by redeeming the place of literature as a genuine expression and articulation of the Holocaust,
but literature can only be a piece of the story. The Holocaust and
how we remember it must become Jewish: it must weave its way
into the theology of lived Jewishness, into ritual and rite, into Jewish
identity in a way that does not require becoming *everything*. Elie Wiesel has famously said that Auschwitz is as important as Sinai. Some
are horrified by this equation; I am not so scandalized. First of all,
by making the comparison Wiesel affirms that Sinai must be central to Jewish consciousness in an ongoing way. But more important: I believe that the theology I have laid out in this book makes a
similar case, or at least creates the foundational system atop which
a similar claim can be made. Sinai is a mythic moment in the Jewish
past in the grandest sense of the word, in which an event narratively
described is directly associated with a commanding legacy. So important is this mythic moment that, as we saw earlier, the rabbis attempted to ensure that all Jews, including converts, would have the
experience "wired" into their memory. Sinai is defining not merely
because it occupied a place in the Jewish historical past, but because
it has taken on mythic significance and because it is the site of the
full integration of memory, commandedness, and peoplehood in
such a holistic way that these constitutive components cannot be
separated from one another.

My objection to Wiesel only lies in his reading of empirical reality: our community does not yet think about these two events the same way, because we very reasonably have not yet been ready to say boldly and baldly that Auschwitz is mythic; and until we do so we cannot wire the experience into Jewish memory, into a widely elastic cultural imagination, and into a commanding voice that defines Jewish behavior in direct ways. Auschwitz can and should move out of historical time and become mythically significant, omnipresent in the sense that it helps define who we are and, more important, lead us to act differently in the world. Can we find the meaning and the narration in Auschwitz so that it emerges from being a crippling historical moment to the commanding place in Jewish identity that can move us forward?

Or, perhaps, there is another possibility. In this chapter I have mostly hovered around a move toward the process of making things whole once again—of getting past discontinuity, or of remaking the historical into the mythic in order to restore a historical event to an appropriate place in our collective consciousness. I fear that without these mechanisms or some permutation thereof we are left in a debilitating post-traumatic stress disorder, to borrow the language of my friend Rabbi Miriam Margles; or inclined to act out, like enfants terribles fleeing Sinai in failure and maligning the Holocaust as over and irrelevant. Perhaps our anxiety has been thus far of the productive kind; when does it become debilitating?

So here is another alternative, one that does not make things easy but also does not resort to easy or programmatic solutions. I wonder what we might do, as a community reckoning with our increasingly scattered collective consciousness, to try to make peace with the brokenness as a permanent state. Could we live with the chasm? Earlier I spoke about Rabbi Yitz Greenberg's theology of brokenness after the Holocaust. Greenberg writes:

> Pluralism is the living together of absolute truths/faiths/systems that have come to know and accept their own limitations, thus making room for the dignity and truth of the other. This broken truth is the future of

truth in a broken world. Rav Nachman of Bratzlav once wrote that there is no heart so whole as a broken heart. After the Shoah, the world will come to know that there is no truth so whole as a broken truth.

Greenberg offers us another body part to reckon with in our operative metaphor, the broken heart; or perhaps we might say the conflicted mind. When Ruth Messinger speaks of the ills of the world and says, as quoted earlier, that we must not allow ourselves the luxury of being overwhelmed, like Greenberg she takes brokenness as both a permanent mandate as well as an impetus for action. Both Greenberg and Messinger make the rabbinic dictum "You are not required to fulfill the task, but neither are you free to desist from it" just slightly less banal, just slightly more motivational: that the catastrophe and our sense of loss feel so pervasive and suffocating to the point of freezing our action, but somehow we must find a wholeness in which the catastrophe is a defining feature so that we can actually become productive beings on the other side.

Perhaps we look too hard for conviction when it comes to making sense of this particular kind of brokenness. One of the central moments in the Book of Esther is when Mordechai goes to Esther to "call in" the reason he placed her in the palace to begin with, asking her to intercede with the king on behalf of the Jews in the face of the genocidal threat. Mordechai says something interesting to Esther: "Who knows whether it was for a moment like this that you acquired the crown." Now, we are inclined to read this as a tongue-in-cheek comment—that of course it was to be able to intercede in such a scenario that Mordechai and Esther so conspired, and in the bigger sense that God made this all happen in order to reckon with this altogether plausible possibility. But what happens when we actually attach the question mark? Who the hell knows why this all played out the way it did? But does lack of knowledge, and ambivalence of underlying understanding, preclude the responsibility we have to act in the here and now?

Maybe the ethical lesson of the twentieth century is nothing more than that courage and value dwell in ambivalence, so long as we are capable of separating out the purposefulness to act from the need to have fixed and stable explanations for everything. This is the paradigm created by Eliezer Berkovits for the survivor generation, when he simultaneously validates the atheistic response of the survivor as well as the expressions of faith by those who walked into the gas chambers. So long as we are not Job and not even Job's brother, wrote Berkovits memorably, we are without either explanation or the ability to evaluate the explanations. Maybe Berkovits should have stretched this potential for ambivalence, and the courage that he attaches to it, beyond the survivor generation itself. Some Jews have dominated the theological discussion of the Holocaust with a sense of absolute conviction, a conviction that accords with the inevitable fundamentalist Jewish choices that accompany these theological views. We do not have to have the chutzpah to know or understand everything; but we do have to do the work—to start, at long last, remembering the Holocaust as part of our Jewishness.

So what is next? I have thus far argued that Jewish memory is defined by its relationship to commandedness, and I have unpacked that commandedness to include a willingness to stay standing in the face of the visually devastating, and to remain active in relationship. The same ethic of Jewish memory must apply here as well. I say this with reverence and humility: the memory of the Holocaust that dominates our landscape and that generates a panic with its imminent disappearance is indeed in trouble, for it is not the Jewish memory that tolerates creativity and selectivity and that commands behavior. Perhaps by necessity, memory of the Holocaust subordinates itself to the precision and empiricism of historicity, but in doing so it takes on history's vulnerability. This memory has become that of intensive chronicling in search of precision, of building colossal superstructures to hold on to tangible artifacts; it is the kind of historically driven memory that does not tolerate variability—or even humanity—in the inevitable imperfection that characterizes memorial literature.

Over the years, there have been attempts to fold the memory of the Holocaust into the traditional narrative, ritual, and liturgical memorial systems of the Jewish past—the yizker bikher, as we saw, but also including a megillah that was written for the Holocaust, selected pieces of liturgical writing, and even a "haggadah" for Yom HaShoah that ritualizes the Holocaust in ways that beggar belief.

Eating potato skins? Cordoning off the children? Perhaps it was just too soon. How can one playact in the presence of survivors without mocking them or being necessarily reductive to a particular theological outcome?

Still, I wonder whether certain kinds of ritualizations—like leaving a corner of the house unpainted—offer the prospect of something bigger and more lasting for Jewish memory of the Holocaust than even warehouses full of recorded testimonials. Much as we should resist the notion that the Holocaust be codified into one particular ethical outcome, the resistance to allowing its memory to dictate our behavior in direct and meaningful ways risks letting it stand out as anomalous compared with other significant events in the Jewish past. The memory that I fear we are losing—not just about the Holocaust, but about our past in general—is the memory that is characterized by translation and interpretation, that is manifest in standing with our feet in the past and with our heads in the present. Are we prepared, as a community, and especially those of us who have never lived it, to start actually remembering the Holocaust in the ways that our tradition instructs? Are we prepared to take on the obligation to remember as we know how, and to obey the commands that will inevitably stem from this most painful remembering?

Our Rabbi Joshua moment might be the Holocaust, but I think it might represent more provocatively and productively the broader rupture of modernity and questioning of assumptions. An abandonment of core principles, values, behaviors, and sources of knowledge and authority are inevitable, as are mad attempts to desperately cling to them in their allegedly pristine form, to fear and ban all attempts to change them. Neither approach entails the right mourning for Jerusalem; in neither will we merit seeing it rebuilt.

# CHAPTER 5

# Teshuva

## RETURNING *as* REIMAGINING

There is a Jewish problem which is humanly soluble:
the problem of the Western Jewish individual who
or whose parents severed his connection with the
Jewish community in the expectation that he would
thus become a normal member of a purely liberal
or of a universal human society and who is naturally
perplexed when he finds no such society. The solution
to his problem is return to the Jewish community, the
community established by the Jewish faith and the
Jewish way of life—*teshubah* (ordinarily rendered by
"repentance") in the most comprehensive sense.
—*Leo Strauss*, Spinoza's Critique of Religion

In this caricature by Leo Strauss, the Jew is a cliché—the last believer in the idea of the universal society and desperately eager to
join it, only to discover, in a moment of great disenchantment, that
it does not exist. The grass only grows greener outside the imposed

or self-imposed ghetto. Strauss's objective in this essay is primarily political, and speaks to the dislocation of the Jew amid the complexity of the twentieth century. Although he makes reference to the religious phenomenon of the repentant, his message speaks more directly to the emerging voice of Jewish particularistic nationalism that we know as Zionism. After all, Zionism was a movement predicated on the idea of return.

This metaphor of *teshuva*, however, usually defined as repentance, has religious and behavioral implications beyond collective political identity; and Strauss's portrayal of the Jewish experience of modernity is suggestive. When Jewish texts talk about returning, when we think about *teshuva* and especially the ubiquitous modern phenomenon of the *ba'al teshuva*—literally "master of repentance," but simply describing the repentant person—we observe a strange paradox: this notion of returning tends to primarily reflect a process experienced by those who never themselves "left" anywhere. This calls to mind our earlier discussion of children born into idolatry, and how the rabbinic tradition imagines that they are innocent of wrongdoing because they have never been inculcated with the memory to know that they are transgressing. We refer to people who make radical life changes toward religious observance as "returning," and in doing so, we become aware of the fundamental covenantal core of what it is to be Jewish. As old an idea as the Torah's teaching that the generation of the golden calf, punished with circumambulating the wilderness for forty years, could not enter the land of Israel but rather yielded to the subsequent generation—who neither experienced the revelation nor rebelled against it—our tradition teaches that historical distance from an event or from a set of choices has no bearing on our intrinsic relationship to its commanding and binding elements. To reacquaint ourselves with knowledge and to rebuild a relationship with a past is a process of returning, even if it seems entirely new, and even as the old becomes new in our eyes and in our hands.

These past two years have provided me with many opportunities to talk to many people about memory. When I speak publicly, my presentations tend to take an academic tone, and purport to be about Jewish collective memory; but I know very well that memory is one of the most personal of subjects for all of us. Our personalities are defined by our memories, by the conscious and unconscious ways in which we take the stuff we experience, process it, and allow it to define our goals and our self-understanding. We all wrestle with our need to both hold on to painful memories and not let them define us, and to grasp firmly the warm memories that we cherish of people and moments we have lost. So I have known in all my lectures and teaching that I am projecting my own wrestling with the past as I espouse this framework, and that the same goes for all my students and conversation partners. I struggle with the realization that using a rigid paradigm like Yerushalmi's, and the focus on collective and shared memory, often obscures the intensity of the individual experiences of alienation and attachment that characterize how we relate to and stand in relationship with those who come before us.

A few encounters from the past couple of years stand out. Once when I was teaching a small group of Jewish adults, I asked the participants to break off into groups of two and talk about their pasts—and specifically, what events had brought them to this moment in their Jewish explorations. I then asked each person to distill one or two critical moments that they heard from their partner and that they thought essential to that person's narrative and to share these examples with the group. Each individual would then hear his or her own experiences narrated by someone else. It was an exercise in memory times two—about how we narrate our own experiences, and about how we hear and narrate the experiences of others. We probed as a group the various discomforts that arose when someone would hear a partner articulating what he or she heard as a critical moment, focusing on something that the narrator had mentioned but perhaps not emphasized, or the surprise in hearing someone interpret a moment from another's past as meaning something different from the meaning assumed by the narrator.

In one case, two women paired off. One was born Jewish, with a long and familiar curriculum vitae of Jewish engagement: from day school through camp, onto activism at Hillel, and now raising children of her own into a similar trajectory. The second was a convert to Judaism with none of these experiences. Although her life experience had surely been rich, this to her paled in relevance compared to the rest of the group and what she considered the exercise. Given the opportunity to speak, this second woman struggled to distill her partner's narrative into a particular moment or experience. What she heard—and what she could not help comparing to her own experience—was not a set of memories but a magnificent tableau of Jewish accomplishment and fulfillment that made her own empty background feel that much more vacant and even threatening. She spoke of her envy of this "memory" that her friend bore, saying that it represented what she has always been seeking and knows she can never actually accumulate. How would she ever catch up? After all, we cannot retry our childhoods.

There is something undeniably sad about this perspective. Envy about a narrative, for someone else's story, is never an appealing trait. I learned from Laura Levitt, a professor of gender studies and Jewish studies, about the "piety problem" that pervades how Jews think about our recent past (and especially the Holocaust) and the public perception that there is a specific and holy story that must be preserved, even if the story is not ours and even if we do not relate to it. Think of the sense of alienation at a tragic moment when you fail to experience the "right" sentiment, or when your own experience does not match that of those around you. This applies not just to the Holocaust—although that is where much of our attention around ownership of a narrative tends to be focused—but to all other Jewish collective and personal narratives as well. The whole notion of narrative, the value we place on how we tell our own unique story, should allow individuals to value their personal experiences of the world, and to minimally hold them together with the cultural expectations of what they are supposed to know or remember, and to find a voice in that process.

But I found this episode sad also because the stories that only converts can tell are often the most fascinating and suggestive moments of personal religious transformation in Jewish life, offering a window into how our tradition and community appear from the outside and a perspective that blends otherness with insiderness in extremely valuable ways. The transformations and acts of boundary crossing inherent in the life of the convert are so much more dramatic than the explorations of born Jews, as the life changes they make have such powerful consequences. So it is unsurprising, if unfortunate, that in the eyes of this woman Camp Ramah flowed together harmoniously and loftily with USY, day school, a Jewish spouse, and so on, as the shared constitutive elements of a "full" Jewish identity and one richer than her own. Yet not only are these experiences no better, objectively, than her own story, they lack the sense of rupture that is often so key to the process of transformation. I was eager to hear this person articulate her own narrative of discovery and self-discovery, in ways that would help us all learn— much as I have learned in listening to one convert friend who talks about being a Jew by choice, with the caveat that the choice was not his own.

The source of this sensation for this student was her unshakable feeling that a Jewish life without personal and communal Jewish memories, especially in the "deep" past, is incomplete and inauthentic. This I blame both on our human nature and on our tendency to conflate our personal stories with the collective, to claim that collective Jewish memory is basically a composite of our own personal narratives. We mistake lived Jewish life for Jewish values. In spite of the Jewish texts I mentioned earlier—all souls at Sinai, e.g.—it is hard to shake the quick and subtle move through which a specific set of Jewish associations and choices appears more authentic than others. This is a similar move that Martin Buber laments in the conflation of religion with religiosity. Religion, the set of norms, expectations, experiences, and ideas that is fixed and is transmitted, does not have the vibrancy of religiosity, which is the creative principle that absorbs and renews this set. When the woman who converted to Judaism hides her past in seeking the box of Jewish normalcy, she has valorized this notion of religion over the creative and transformative force that is clearly alive within her, that motivated her to leave her land, her birthplace, the house of her parents to cling to the Jewish people. She valorizes a specific tradition—in this case, the legacy of Jewish institutional life—over the basic *value* of tradition, which is its ability to bind the vibrancy of personal experience and the creative impulse together with continuity to the past.

In my case: I think a lot about a photograph that is somewhere in my parents' house (which itself has always been a moving target). The photo depicts my two brothers and me, when I was about age four, sitting around a recently lit Hanukkah menorah, in our pajamas with damp hair from a bath. We are all smiling in that amazing way that only childhood photos can convey, encapsulating a childhood and freezing what was likely a chaotic evening with three boys under age six and turning it into a tableau of happiness and serenity. I don't remember posing for the picture, much less the evening or the celebration of Hanukkah that preceded the photograph. But the photograph creates a different kind of visualized memory, so that when I think about Hanukkah in my childhood I feel some element of the warmth of the towel after the bath, the cleanness, the water in my ears. Hanukkah is a holiday of commemoration, but I tend to remember Hanukkahs past more than I can remember an ancient internecine conflict or an implausible miracle. This is personal memory transformed into an anchor for Jewish engagement and participation, and it is undeniably effective; after all, I want my own children's memories of Jewish life in our home to also feel warm and happy. Beyond this one photo and that one episode, when I think about my upbringing, I can remember the sense of all the holidays and Shabbat celebrations in our house; but that memory has become a composite *feeling*, a disconnected and thus strange emotional relationship to the past—rather than an identifiable set of images or mechanically understood experiences.

Scientists now tend to believe that the brain does not preserve memory as a camera or a photocopier would, but instead by preserving bits and pieces of an event or person, and relying on our ability to do the work of stitching the pieces back into a coherent image. These fragments rely on stimuli to be reconstituted. When we do things that jog our memory—hear a story retold, see a photograph, or even have a sensory experience peripheral to the actual memory but still evocative of it—we are able to take the connected fragment in our brain and reconstruct the narrative around it. Of course, in this process the line between memory and original narrative is blurred; think of what our brains do in organizing the material from our dreams when we wake up, or how children claim to remember things that they only know from narratives overheard from their parents. There is an unmarked but retrospectively obvious threshold between actual memories and the stories we tell ourselves. We do not speak aloud the processes in which we think; our mouth translates into organized words a much more complex and sophisticated system of ideas and experiences that our brain continually generates. Our brains apply a fundamental organizing principle to take all this sensory data, these shards of memory, and tell stories or form sentences.

It is because of this gap between memory and storytelling that we can experience accidental "memory distortions," wherein our associations mislead us to believe we experienced something because our rational systems have intuitively interpreted experiences in a certain way. In one example, the memory theorist Daniel Schacter describes reading people a list of words: "candy, sour, sugar, bitter, good, taste, tooth, nice, honey, soda, chocolate, heart, eat, cake, pie." He subsequently documents how frequently those tested afterward insist that the word "sweet" was included in the list. The interpretive act of giving coherence and meaning to the list leads people to remember something they did not hear. This is in part one legacy of Freud and a cautionary tale to those who dabble in managing the memories of others; the work of reassembling the fragments or broken pieces may lead to creating a previously unknown image that purports to be an authentic memory. I suspect the contemporary Jewish alienation from the past stems from a different set of significant causes—sometimes the malicious disassembling of the past, sometimes apathy, and sometimes just this lack of self-confidence that what we are remembering is really right, and an anxiety that then emerges on how that memory should hold any sway over us.

I am then able to analyze what this Hanukkah photograph does for me: I don't remember the episode as much as identify with its story. The image enables me to stand in relationship to everything it depicts—my family, my faith, my upbringing, and, most important, the deep emotional resonances that tie all of these together. The photograph "jogs my memory" in that it creates an evocative narrative in which I feature and belong, and it generates continuity between my current and past choices. This continuity, after all, is what memory is entirely about.

Now: what do we make of memories or experiences that we never actually had? This question, to which we have been building, goes to the heart of a project that aims for a restoration of what I have been calling "memory." And the challenge here is astonishing: we know that meaningful memory—which will entail a bridge between past and present, which will foster a deeper sense of Jewish authenticity and purposefulness and a restoration of confident Jewish self-consciousness not merely in the face of but in concert with the challenges of modernity—that this memory, like all memory, will entail a creative combination of fragments of knowledge together with a generative and connective mythic narrative framework. What does it look like to build this bridge, when on hand we increasingly lack the fragmentary pieces of the past, as well as the narration that connects us to it—and perhaps even the skills that Jews have long had to generate that narration?

And I continue to think about this photograph: as an encoded emotional trigger moment that consciously and unconsciously informs my adult choices, this worked for me. But it did not work for all the members of my family—or perhaps it was overridden by other equally salient memories—and it is obviously and transparently insufficient. If the ruptures of modern Jewish life that I have discussed so far are real and as significant as I have depicted, then the solutions must involve a greater degree of repair work than we currently do. The answer to make Judaism a part of home life, to make specific educational choices for our children, these tactical decisions create positive personal memory and are thus worthwhile; but they must not be thought to substitute for a deep collective process. Herein lies the urgency of the problem: collective mythic memory is too important to be subordinated to the personal memories and baggage that we all schlep around, and too deep for simply programmatic or organizational thinking.

Thus far I have talked about awe, and how we use our eyes; love and the mechanics of the heart; commandment, a tool that drives our hands and feet in the service of obligation; and the challenges of dissonance that wreak havoc on our brain. A key theme of twentieth century Jewish thought has been the imagined provision of "therapy" for the damaged Jewish soul and psyche—Zionism, to be sure, the writings of Franz Rosenzweig on *Understanding the Sick and the Healthy*, and many others—and I suppose my effort here is no different. I see these different body parts representing portions of the body Israel, and desperately in need of a restorative paradigm to stand together again, to be able to manifest metaphorically the words of the psalmist that "All my bones will declare—God! Who is like you!" The essential last body parts that need definition are those that provide structure, such as the skeletal system or connective tissue that holds the body together; or perhaps in a book about memory they are the neural networks that keep information going to and coming from the metaphorical hippocampus where all the data is stored.

Here I want to elaborate on this idea that *teshuva* is the core principle of restoration that can help us reestablish the collective-holistic Jewish experience of modernity. I am not the first to make this claim. Emil Fackenheim, at the end of his *To Mend the World*, discusses the instinct by many modern Jewish thinkers toward rehabilitating *teshuva*; and perhaps my reading that follows owes an intellectual debt to Fackenheim's bridging of the new and the old as the basic paradigm that I am trying to build.

*Teshuva* is a troubling word. Its associations connote a specific set of commitments and changes, invariably now associated with a specific kind of religiosity. In this problematic understanding, *teshuva* is a kind of retrograde package of regret and transformative change, the strategy by which we attempt to undermine the folly of past choices and our original selves in the process. This is especially the case when we think about *teshuva* as an individual exercise. The dramatic display of chest-beating and mournful laments that characterizes the repentant liturgy amplifies the centrality of human failure in this work of alleged "return," suggesting that we somehow become whole only by becoming incomplete, frail shells of our former selves.

Maimonides applies a creative literalism to the word *teshuva* in explaining how perfect repentance comes about. It is not that a sinner can reverse the sin, nor that regret alone undoes the misdoing. According to Maimonides, perfect repentance is achieved when the sinner encounters the same scenario in which he transgressed, under identical circumstances, and alters his behavior.

In this explanation, perhaps *teshuva* describes less the changed act and more the humility in the willingness to literally return to identical circumstances in which one had previously failed. This alone requires a maturity that reflects a transformed consciousness. Often we avoid the places or circumstances of our regret; we suppress those memories. The idea alone of revisiting places of failure, much less finding the wherewithal to succeed in these environments, indicates sufficient merit of an evolved person. This alone merits the rewards of having undone the wrong, or at least reclaims the reputation of the malfeasant.

The collective process of repentance is trickier, even though at its core the language of repentance originates in Jewish tradition primarily in reference to the collective. The biblical scholar Jacob Milgrom describes Yom Kippur as a "day of purgation," an almost sanitation-oriented festival of washing away the sins of the people of Israel in the Temple. At the center of the liturgy, after all, are the ritual of the sacrificial goat—the literal dispatching of the people's sins away and into the wilderness—and the entry of the high priest to the Holy of Holies to burn incense and restore a sweet savor to the sanctuary. Far removed from the meditative, introspective sensibility wrought by the evolving mores of personal prayer, the biblical process of repentance hinged on the collective willingness of the people to reestablish the purity of their holy place.

Beyond the ritual dimensions, in the prophetic tradition the language of *teshuva* also applied to the collective, and represented the hopes and dreams of the people of Israel to experience a restoration of the divine-human relationship and the storehouse of united sovereignty. The last gasp of the prophetic moment in Jewish history, in the last codified prophetic book of the Bible, when the prophet had become so diminished that he lost his name and merely became "Malachi"—my messenger—comes in the desperate pleading of *shuva elai, v'ashuva alehem*—return to me, and I shall return to you. Here in this dialogical moment stand the people of Israel and God, locked in a troubled relationship of codependency. Elsewhere in the biblical literature the relationship is even more vexed—who does the returning? In Psalms, in a piece of text that has become liturgized, we ask God to return us—to actively make us return—

thus exonerating ourselves from the responsibility of taking that first step. Indeed, so much of the tensions around Jewish nationalism that persist in the contemporary Jewish community derive from this theological ambiguity: whose responsibility is the restoration? Who is supposed to return first—God or the people? In this dialogical relationship, who takes the first step?

But the issue is even more complex as we think about the ramifications of this imagined restoration. Does restoration involve a retrojection of values? A model of returning to outmoded ideals, to a world from which we have evolved—such a scenario would be wildly uncompelling, though certainly a strong segment of the Jewish community, the ultra-Orthodox, strives to at least freeze time if not to restore some elements of a lost past world. This view is not merely aesthetically, morally, and culturally uncompelling; it also does not represent Jewish tradition and values with regard to the meaning of restoration. In Jewish language, restoration involves seeking and aspiring for a transformed world that never actually existed. This model is paradoxical and suggestive—we talk about going back to a place in which we never were, either as individuals or as a collective.

Our only means to do this is through our deep understanding of memory, a memory that takes pieces of the past—voluntarily, selectively—and threads them with a narrative that connects to our present. This thread enables us to move forward even though it appears we are moving backward, generating exactly the kinetic energy suggested in the terminology of *shuva* but toward an active, forward, and progressive vision that the urgency of the texts' uses suggests. The oddity of the prophetic legacy in the Bible is that the ambitious and socially just agenda of the woebegone prophets was not something they could actually look back on longingly. Nowhere in the story of the Bible is the ideal and idyllic city of God and community of covenant ever convincingly constituted. The prophets used the language of the past to advance a novel, radical vision for the present because it undergirded that vision with a specific kind of force, perhaps the force of precedent: We *were* great once, now we can be great again. Remember? And of course the fragments are there for that false but inspirational memory—the pieces of the biblical tradition that speak of the imperative to care for the widow and orphan, the narratives that express God's extraordinary compassion in dialectic with judiciousness—to convey strong words and sensibilities: we have faced these challenges before and were capable together of overcoming them.

I have been using a metaphor of body and self to talk about these core concepts of Jewishness, and at the same time I am attempting to think about these categories as defining the collective experience. A paradigm of Jewish thought that merely reiterates the notion of the "sovereign self," but that does not challenge us to think about what binds us together, concedes a great and irrevocable loss to modernity; it grants to Jewish diversity a primacy to the element of diversity rather than the Jewishness.

Some of the current rhetoric in the Jewish community around what is called "peoplehood" starts—as my colleague and friend Eliyahu Stern wonderfully demonstrates—from the self-destructive standpoint of trying to describe and define everyone in the Jewish spectrum, to attract and incorporate every diverse manifestation of contemporary Jewishness. This stems ironically from an act of self-preservation, from the desire to construct a mutually agreeable big tent that is nonexclusionary. On one level, it is simply silly: what are meaningful boundaries if everyone is inside of them, if they do not achieve any means of self-differentiation?

But this approach is also untenable. A parable: Jewish diversity may be compared to dozens of marbles scattered over the floor, marbles of different colors, shapes, sizes; in different parts of the room, some still moving, some close together and some very far apart. They are all marbles, to be sure, but only because the word *marble* describes all of them; they have obvious differences, and the more that each resembles a different marble in the room, the more its differences to totally different marbles become clear. Some of the current projects on peoplehood appear to be trying to define the class of marbles in the room. They do so by trying to place a boundary around all the marbles, to create a paradigm that incorporates all this difference. It is extremely difficult to pull this off: the marbles are still moving, and the definitional process—when applied to such a wildly diverse pool—becomes watered-down and arbitrary. Nor does it effectively account for manifestations we have yet to see—marbles that are still in the bag, marbles that move out of the room. Jewish identity is so kinetic and creative that a project that defines all of what is out there will need constant revision over time.

Instead: what if we thought about the Jewish collective not with reference to the scattered marbles on the floor but rather by describing the sack of marbles before it opened up, and before the marbles all came crashing down? What was the commonality of their experience then, what held them together, how could they be described in their more static moment? Perhaps the unifying and defining qualities of the disparate Jewish people lie in the places of origin, the formative moments, the source from which the diversity generated. The marbles do not become any less diverse in this analogy, for they were as different in the bag as they are now on the floor. Ancient, medieval, early modern Jewish history entailed a dramatic diversity, and many contemporary manifestations of diverse Jewish expression can trace an authentic line back to a historical kernel. Still, this diversity stemmed from a shared sense of original place, from a core sense of binding—a binding that once let out of the bag is difficult to sense as well as to restore. The historian Jacob Katz describes the transition to modernity as a "breakdown of traditional society as a whole," as manifested in the ability to question everything previously considered axiomatic—assumptions about social class and standing, professional roles, ideas and ideals, attitudes toward institutions. Jewish diversity flowered in the ability to reject the systems that held the collective together yet still identify, in one way or another, with a collective that was losing any sense of identity and definition. So the sack of marbles ruptured.

Still, it should be easier to describe ourselves when we think back to whence we came, rather than trying to account for all the complex ways in which we have evolved. This is, I think, at the core of the process and theology of restoration—our attempt to once again give definition to and reprioritize the values of our collective, and to try to allow them to define us more effectively.

Part of the reason I like this marble metaphor is that imagining how wildly the marbles fall and disperse speaks to the speed and unpredictability of how Jewishness has responded to modernity and diversified as a result. This response seems particularly dramatic in light of the traditional ideas of transmission and reception—*masoret* and *kabbalah*—that I discussed in my introduction as the core symbolic framework in which Jews imagined the sequence of ideas, values, and authority. *Change* has always been a contentious process in Jewish history, as in any traditionalist framework; not because things are not constantly changing but because the changers must preserve a thin line between the overhaul they are doing and the public perception of continuity. When the contemporary Jewish community talks about continuity, as it does quite frequently, it risks creating a hollow continuity for continuity's sake, a continuity that tends to be championed by and manifest in institutions rather than ideas, in stability rather than values. Why do we trust our own impetuousness so much to think that our specific choices should be replicated by our children?

Two separate aspects of the way we tend to talk about continuity are flawed. First, we make so few demands on ourselves as Jews but somehow expect that those who follow us will replicate our fundamentally, idiosyncratically self-justified choices. The Israeli author David Grossman writes that "throughout all our history we survived in order to live, and now we are living in order to survive." As David Hartman often says, what is continuity without content?

Second, we mistake innovative and transformative Jewish creativity in younger Jews that takes place outside conventional Jewish institutions as equivalent to the rejection of Jewishness modeled by unaffiliated or disaffected Jews. My grandfather, Jacob Doppelt, was a Jewish builder, part of that Greatest Generation who lived through a depression and the Second World War, who built a business, a family, and a number of significant and—by today's standards—decidedly mainstream Jewish institutions. He died way too young, though perhaps it gave some comfort to my grandmother to see a young man (my younger brother) who was a direct beneficiary of these institutions—synagogue, day school, Israel—grow up bearing his name. I wonder sometimes about my grandfather's parents (whom I never knew) as well as his children (like my mother), and the wavy way in which the building of institutions and the use of those institutions depend on each other. There are times to build, and times to make use of that building. I cannot imagine my great-grandparents shaking their heads in dismay as my grandfather used his resources to build a Jewish day school, even though that institution was previously unknown to the community. Nor can I imagine that my grandfather would have been disappointed, had he lived long enough, to see our graduation from a day school that my parents had not themselves founded. Jewish continuity depends on discontinuity; it needs generations of builders, and generations of clients, and perhaps some of the intergenerational tension that currently populates the Jewish world is our wrestling with this basic truth of change as a vehicle for survival.

So meaningful continuity requires discontinuity; or, more accurately, continuity probably should resemble a sine curve rather than a straight line. Managing continuity in relating past to present has played an essential role in Jewish thought. As we discussed earlier, this notion of tradition does not erase the multiplicity of narratives and the possibility that new pasts emerge in the future. I do not see in Rabbi Joshua's stance, even with its specific legal prescriptions, the affirmation of only one sacred past. It is rather a philosophical system that enables that very possibility to emerge. Michael Meyer, a modern Jewish historian, addresses the challenges of talking about "continuity" when it comes to studying and analyzing Jewish history. Is there really one story? The migrations, dispersals, and variations in Jewish experience make it difficult to create one continuous narrative, leading some skeptical scholars to suggest that there is no such thing as Jewish history except as an ideological construct. Meyer's answer is to offer a different model of continuity using a metaphor of a string made up of many interwoven threads: there can be continuity from the beginning of the string to the end, even if threads in the string start and stop, and even if there is discontinuity among the various threads along the way.

This is the means by which a historian makes sense of a conflicted reality, by which he looks at the breadth of Jewish experience from Baghdad to Berlin and attempts to see a meaningful cross-cultural story. Equally important for our purposes is the retrospective system in which we take stock of the place where we are standing and work backward, deciphering which threads formed part of the string that connects our past to our present.

The historian and critic David Lowenthal differentiates between heritage and history in a way that echoes Yerushalmi's distinction between memory and history, in service of a broader cultural critique about the ways we memorialize. His point resonates with what I have written here: the proliferation of museums, of collecting the past, is comparably useless to the zealots whom Rabbi Joshua attacks here in the earlier text. Both represent opposite fundamentalist responses to the legacy of the past—the former in trying to hold on to it without allowing it to dictate behavior in the present, the latter in totally crippling that very behavior. The conclusion of the Rabbi Joshua text hints at the radical complexity of Rabbi Joshua's approach: those who mourn the trauma of Jerusalem will merit to share in her joy. Certainly the zealous students who almost stopped eating and drinking should qualify for this status! The nuance in this text is found in the suggestion that mourning for the past is not the same as dwelling in it. And, not surprisingly, the text itself is also about *teshuva*, about restoration in the deepest sense: it imagines a way out of the past toward a redemptive future, even as it grapples with how to make sense of it. This echoes a familiar biblical and rabbinic trope about catastrophe and redemption—those who sow with tears will reap with joy; the one who is truly wise sees the processes of restoration unfolding even during the periods of destruction.

Even without core beliefs that have been shattered, even with a false past, even without a tether that commits us to communal choices, geographic boundaries, ideological frames, there exists the potential for a meaningful Jewish authenticity. Authenticity is measured on two axes: the extent to which we feel authentic to ourselves, and the extent to which the things we do feel authentic as compared to what we think we are supposed to be doing. The latter measure entails our subordinating our activities to the scrutiny of an arbitrary sense of what Jewishness is supposed to be or look like. In the quest for authenticity, sometimes one of these metrics of authenticity trumps the other. So a person may feel inauthentic making traditional choices whether he feels that his ethical impulses are too strong to coexist with those choices or that to make those choices would make him feel inauthentic to himself. Conversely, a person might also feel inauthentic if she were to suppress her intuited beliefs about the world in order to live as part of a community that seems to express a more authentic type of Judaism, since here "authentic" appears to exist only in some abstract, perhaps aesthetically defined way. Neither of these acts of suppression is particularly comfortable.

My goal here is not to revitalize the category of "authenticity," which has been critiqued at length, nor, in the words of Stuart Charme, to prop it up as a means to link us "into conformity with . . . authority" as the politics of authenticity sometimes incline us to do. Instead I am hovering about the problem of our being today so different from one another, so removed from our past and who we might have been, and wondering whether there are ways of adjusting our understanding of that past.

In the story with which I opened this chapter, I lamented how the experience of a convert led her to question the legitimacy of her own narrative. In doing so, I noted how deeply connected rupture and transformation can be: moments of rupture enable us to strategically identify what to take with us and what to leave behind, to become whole with the past as we move into a transformed future. This is the essence of *teshuva*, and the reason the classical rabbis threatened anyone who dared mock the repentant by recalling his past life, and why they valorized so emphatically the position of the convert and the *ba'al teshuva* in Jewish society. *Teshuva* returns us individually and collectively to a wholeness of self and a wholeness of peoplehood—it is the willful affirmation of wholeness in the face of the self-evidently broken.

# CHAPTER 6

# Enlightenment

## A PARABLE

The enlightened will shine like the radiance of the sky,
and those who lead many to righteousness,
like the stars forever and ever
—Daniel 12:3, and the opening to the Zohar

A tale is told in the Talmud:

Babylonian Talmud, Tractate *Hagigah* (14a)
The Rabbis taught: Four entered the "Orchard" (*pardes*) and these are they: ben Azzai, and ben Zoma, The Other (*acher*) and Rabbi Akiva. Rabbi Akiva said to them: "When you arrive at the pure marble stones, don't say, 'Water! Water!,' for it is written: 'A speaker of lies shall not abide before my eyes.'" (Psalms 101:7)
Ben Azzai glimpsed and died; about him it is written: "Precious in the eyes of God is the death of his saints." (Psalms 116:15)
Ben Zoma glimpsed and was affected; and about him it is written, "You have found honey—eat your fill, lest you overeat and vomit." (Proverbs 25:16)

The Other cut the roots.

Rabbi Akiva departed in peace.

"The Other cut the roots," and about him it is written, "Let not your mouth bring sin upon your flesh (Eccl. 5:5)." And what was it? He saw that Metatron was given permission to sit and write down the merits of Israel. He said: "We learned that in heaven there is no sitting, and no competition, and no necks, and no exhaustion—perhaps (heaven forbid) there are two powers."

They removed Metatron from his place and beat him with sixty pillars of fire. They said to him: "When you saw him, how come you didn't stand before him?" They gave him permission to wipe away the merits of The Other; and a voice came out and said, "Return, wayward sons (Jer. 3:22)—except for The Other." He said, "Since that man was banished from that world, let him enjoy this one"—and The Other went out to *tarbut ra'ah* [polluted practice]. He went to a prostitute and solicited her trade. She said, "Are you not Elisha son of Avuyah?" He pulled out a radish from the ground on Shabbat and gave it to her. She said, "It must be another."

The Other (after he had strayed to *tarbut ra'ah*) asked Rabbi Meir: "What does it mean when it says, 'Also this one, in opposition/correlation to the other one, was made by God?' (Eccl. 7:14)" He said to him, "To everything that God created, he created something else that correlated—he created mountains, he created hills; he created seas, he created rivers." He said to him: "Your teacher Rabbi Akiva did not say that. Rather, he created righteous people, he created wicked people; he created the garden of Eden, he created Gehenna. Each and every person has two halves—one in the garden of Eden and one in Gehenna. When the righteous person triumphs, he takes his own and his friend's portion in the garden of Eden; when the wicked is found culpable, he takes his own and his friend's portion in Gehenna.". . .

The Other (after he had strayed to *tarbut ra'ah*) asked of Rabbi Meir: "What does it mean when it says, 'Gold and glass cannot approximate its worth, nor its exchange in gold vessels?'" (Job 28:15) He said to him, "These are words of Torah, that are as difficult to acquire as gold and gilded vessels, but are as easily lost as glass vessels." He said to him: "Your teacher Rabbi Akiva did not say that. Rather, with glass and gold vessels, just as if they break there is a remedy; so too, a Torah scholar.

Even if he sours, there is a remedy." He said to him: "So you too, return!" He said: "I have already heard from behind the partition, 'Return wayward sons—except for the Other.'"

The Rabbis taught: There was a story involving The Other, who was riding a horse on the Sabbath, and Rabbi Meir was walking behind him to learn Torah from his mouth. He said to him, "Meir, go back—for I have calculated through the footsteps of my horse that the Sabbath boundary ends here." Rabbi Meir said to him: "So you too go back!" He said to him, "Did I not already tell you? I have already heard from beyond the partition, 'Return, wayward sons—except for The Other.'" He grabbed him and pulled him to the house of study. He said to a child, "Tell me your lesson." He said, "There is no peace, said God, for the wicked (Is. 48:22)." He brought him to a different synagogue. He said to a child, "Teach me your lesson." He said to him, "Though you may wash with niter and use much soap, the stain of your iniquity remains before me (Jer. 2:22)." He brought him to another synagogue. He said to a child, "Teach me your lesson. He said, "And you, ruined one, what will you do? Though you wear crimson clothes, don garments of gold, paint your eyelids, it is for naught that you beautify yourself (Jer. 4:30)." He brought him to another synagogue, until he had brought him to thirteen synagogues—and in all of them they taught lessons like these. To the last one he said, "Teach me your lesson." The boy said, "And to the wicked God said, "For what purpose do you speak of my laws (Ps. 50:16)?" That boy used to stutter when speaking, and it sounded like he said, "And to Elisha God said . . ." There are some who say that he had a knife in his hand and he tore him to pieces and sent them to the thirteen synagogues; others say that he said, "If I had a knife in my hand, I would have torn him apart."

When The Other died, they said: "We cannot pass judgement against him, and we cannot allow him to the world to come. We cannot pass judgement against him, because he engaged in Torah study. And we cannot allow him to the world to come because he sinned." Rabbi Meir said: "It is better that he should be judged, and then be allowed to enter the world to come. When I die, I will raise smoke from his grave." When Rabbi Meir died, a pillar of smoke arose from The Other's grave. Rabbi Yochanan said: "Is it a great accomplishment to burn one's teacher? He was among us, and we were not able to save him. If I take him by the hand, who will take him away from me?" Rabbi Yochanan went on: "When I die, I will extinguish the smoke from his grave." When Rabbi Yochanan died, the pillar of smoke from The Other's grave stopped. A certain eulogist said about him: "Even the guardian of the gate did not stand before you, our teacher!"

The architects of the Talmud cite this legendary and esoteric account as part of their commentary on the very mishnah we discussed in the section on awe, on those matters we are forbidden from looking at and the realms of problematic knowledge. In this tragic tale, the metaphor of seeing characterizes all of the experiences of the different sages in the orchard. Although the verbs describing what ben Zoma, ben Azzai, and Aher see differ, each figure suffers some perilous fate on the basis of troubled seeing. Only Rabbi Akiva escapes, and only Rabbi Akiva is described as not looking.

In this narrative, Akiva is also unique for another reason: he speaks to his colleagues, and offers a warning. The warning relates less to what they will see, and more to what they should not do in that moment of seeing. When you reach that place, when you see whatever astonishing thing these pure marble stones represent, do not exclaim, "Water! Water!" The proof text Akiva cites reinforces the core message: speaking will mean lying. Simply put, you will interpret what you see as something that it is not, and that speaking will make a liar of you. Akiva seems to know exactly what the consequences of seeing are—namely, a kind of necessary miscomprehension. Somehow Akiva appears to know the secrets of the *pardes*, and the key to survival within.

What is this *pardes*, this mysterious paradise, orchard, Edenic garden that makes wise men fall as dramatically as those who fell in the primordial paradise lost—but here not in battles on the plain of heaven but in seeing completely inorganic sights? The Jewish interpretive tradition is rich on this question, with interpretations ranging from the *pardes* representing a version of paradise to standing in as either a specific or generic metaphor for esoteric or Torah knowledge. These readings are all probably right, but we are remiss to ignore the verdant literalism of the orchard as a key piece of the story, and how the suggestive actions of planting, sowing, reaping, uprooting make fuller sense when we focus on the orchard as both real and symbolic.

Two of the main figures never seem to have the opportunity to make this core mistake of misinterpreting what they see. Ben Zoma and ben Azzai, their parallel names making them parallel literary characters, see something—and before they can react, their very act of seeing brings about their demise. One sees and dies, evidently collapsing under the weight of what he cannot comprehend. Another sees and is "affected." The subsequent narrative in the Talmud describes ben Zoma's apparent insanity, or perhaps social marginalization, or both. In the Talmud's example, he becomes fixated on an insoluble problem, so much so that he becomes immune and alien to social encounters, his head in the clouds, dwelling on the margins. Alas, says his teacher—ben Zoma is on the outside, looking in. The abortive story of these two sages ends here.

It is only the sage Elisha son of Avuyah who falls victim to Akiva's warning: he sees one thing, and interprets aloud what he sees. What does he see? The Talmud says that he sees a seated angel doing things Elisha does not expect to see in the divine pantheon. God and God's retinue do not look like they are supposed to look. Now this does not exactly comport with Akiva's warning, for Elisha does not see pure marble stones and does not exclaim "Water!" but it reflects the same challenge. It is a midrash on a midrash. When you see something challenging, provocative, you may be inclined to resort to your analytical frameworks—the way you have learned before, the way you understand things—to process, unpack, or explain the problem. Earlier we talked about cognitive dissonance, the theory that suggests that our inability to hold conflicting ideas or propositions in our head inevitably inclines us to resolve the dissonance by eliminating one of the ideas. Here, Elisha stands conflicted: either what he knows about heaven—(through his Jewish education?)—is false or something is amiss in what he is seeing. We tend to believe what we see, and Elisha is no exception. "You *saw* what I did to Egypt!" You see the seams of the biblical text that you have believed, you see the flaws in your parents and grandparents, you see the problems that have befallen your ancestors in their parochial naivete. Perhaps, Elisha says aloud, what I knew about heaven was wrong and there are actually two powers in heaven. Perhaps there is no singularity to this one particular truth that I have been taught. This moment of heresy violates Akiva's warning to keep silent, and badly so; in the narrative, Elisha is still standing in the "paradise" when he offers this devastating interpretation. His words inflict damage on the paradise itself, and we understand that this is one way in which he is "cutting the shoots." Standing in the divine orchard, he is actually uprooting it, his piercing words shattering the vision held together by what he had considered true. Rabbi Rehume falls from the roof and dies.

But is Elisha's sin here so hard to understand, or his failure a matter to which we should not be sympathetic? Akiva demands of Elisha one of two options, neither of which is easy or palatable. One option, the fundamentalist option that he embodies, involves not looking. Enter paradise, perhaps, whatever that means—the world of enlightenment (do not fruits of knowledge grow there?), the world of mystical seeking, the increasingly esoteric place of deep understanding—but if you want to walk out, be careful what you look at. What kind of adventure is that? When I have taught this text to young Jewish students, I have met deep resistance to this Akiva and to the pedestal in Jewish tradition on which he is placed. Our cultural seduction with knowledge for its own sake, with the value of the adventure and the seeking that comes with it, makes us inevitably skeptical of those who would place blinders on our eyes along that voyage. Is survival alone within the system sufficient enough incentive to miss out on the magnificent things there are to see outside?

Of course, Akiva's narrative must be more complicated than that. After all, Akiva knows what there is to see, and what not to say in that moment. How does he know this? Our most obvious guess is that *Akiva has been there before*. Like any great guide, he has learned—perhaps through trial and error—what to do and what not to do along the way, the shortcuts and passageways. And yet as a tour guide, Akiva must be evaluated as hopeless. Three of his fellow travelers fail to come back. We might blame them for their failings, but we must linger in the moment that the chaperone—the travelers' teacher, after all—bears some culpability in this account. Akiva emerges whole, but sullied in his own way.

I wonder whether the pedestal on which Akiva lives in the rabbinic corpus—the most exceptional of all rabbis, a man considered most knowledgeable and closest to the divine but who only began his learning in the middle of his life—is a subtle means of marginalizing Akiva as well. Akiva becomes infallible in the traditional imagination, in part because his behavior is incomprehensible, and at the cost of learning from that behavior. We sometimes do this to people, enviously or hopelessly elevating those to whom we cannot relate, those whose skills or capacities are beyond our reach. In the process, we ultimately identify more with those who fall short.

So if "not seeing" is one unpalatable option, the other difficult option is the stance of dissonance. In this reading, Akiva demands of Elisha that he inhabit the *pardes* and see things that defy explanation—and still that he resist the temptation to explain them through recourse to the knowledge he previously held. In other words, he asks of Elisha to suspend the mechanisms by which human beings learn and live. When we learn, we process and accumulate; we use what we know, the skills and vocabulary, to digest and interpret what we see and come across. Actually, we depend on this process. We depend on our memories to enable us to interpret and absorb new information. The language Elisha uses to process this new information is so telling—"We learned," he says. This is the perfect student moment, as he encounters a new and unexpected reality and replays what he has learned in order to process and integrate the new information.

But Elisha's learning fails him. Akiva's warning demands dissonance, and asks Elisha to simultaneously hold on to his learning—his previously held knowledge—and to stand facing this jarring reality, and to hold the two together in a perilous silence. I would suggest that this is both a virtually impossible task as well as an extremely common and contemporary challenge. Every time we learn something new or encounter a new reality we experience some minor dissonance as it settles into place among our more firmly held knowledge and assumptions. This kind of dissonance and friction is highly desirable. But the more dramatic dissonance is a hallmark of the Jewish experience of modernity, the inevitable and unresolved conflict between those things we learn and those things we see, the systems of Jewish belief and the experiences of modern reality. The notion that we would hold, freeze, stand in a suspended dissonance seems both impossible and highly desirable—and reflects perhaps the exact "failure" at the core of Elisha's experience in the *pardes*. The disappointment of this text lies in finding that Elisha is human, but not superhuman.

And so, thankfully, as we see here and further on, the text is extremely ambivalent about Elisha's sin or "heresy." The first character to be properly punished in the text is not Elisha but the angel Metatron himself, who failed to meet Elisha's expectations. This is an astonishing comment: the Talmud suggests that although the heavenly realms may reflect truths unknown or unfathomable to humans, they are obligated to undertake a kind of *hesed*, an act of kindness, to adapt their appearance to avoid the foibles of fallible humans. The dissonance of incompatible truths can be avoided if one of the truths hides its true nature. But after Metatron is punished, so too is Elisha. A heavenly voice emerges—"Return, wayward sons—except for you." This devastating voice echoes with the deeply human experience of alienation that tends to believe that it alone experiences loss from the otherwise solid and cohesive human collective. We miss a truth of the modern Jewish experience when we narrate the blessed traumas of emancipation and enlightenment only as applicable to the collective. It is not only a collective dissonance that we experience as Jews in the modern world, but so many individual heartbreaks, and each is rooted in a singular experience. Elisha hears a heavenly voice that speaks directly to him, like every teenager or college student who feels that suddenly the foundations of her world are shaking. Perhaps that system is okay for the others, that voice enables him to say to himself; perhaps they, after these experiences, after these shocking sights, can return. Not me; my door is closed. The rabbinic commentaries that vehemently maintain that this closing of the door was legally legitimate, predicated on *Aher's* sinfulness or perhaps on God's prophetic foreknowledge that Elisha would not return, miss the pathos of the story. Wanton or accidental, that closure brings pain, especially in the voice that Elisha tells us that he hears.

Indeed, a related midrash uses the same terminology—"cutting the shoots"—in describing the original "fall" from paradise in the Garden of Eden. The midrash teases out and exposes the differences between how God threatened Adam not to eat of the tree and how Eve recounted the same prohibition to extend to even *touching* the tree. The midrash supplies the narrative according to which the serpent pushed Eve into the tree; and upon showing her that mere contact with the tree did not result in her death, the serpent was able to coax her into eating of the fruit as well. The midrash uses this text to warn that the parameters that we create around that which is prohibited should not exceed the prohibition itself, lest one fall and "cut the shoots." This phrasing sadly evokes Elisha; was his stumble, too, an accident? Surely one cannot unsee that which has become exposed; willful blinding, Oedipus learns, does not unmake the negative image in the mind. In fact, herein the Mishnah's warnings that one who sees and acts unmercifully regrets his own birth are so much more accurate than even the Bible's warning of death for eating of the tree of knowledge. Adam and Eve may acquire mortality, but it accompanies the divinity and immortality that their knowledge and capacity to choose bestow upon them. Franz Kafka points out the bitterness that comes with the unfettering yielded by knowledge, the desire evident in the very phraseology of calling it "the fall" to unlearn or unknow or to at least restrict that knowledge to something less than the totality of one's experience. Enlightenment and discovery—whether accidental, deliberate, inevitable—brings with it as much sadness and loss as excitement and growth.

And Rabbi Kook picks up this terminology as well to caution that "wisdom alone, devoid of the aim of the fear of God, is meaningless"—that it is considered the "cutting of the shoots." One might read this as blaming Elisha for foraying into knowledge unprepared; one might also say Elisha, like many of us, has not the equipment or the tools to know what that fear of God is supposed to look like.

"If there is no God, everything is permitted"—and so Elisha departs the orchard, perhaps forlorn, perhaps feeling rejected, and takes new ownership of his world in the most coarse and carnal ways possible. In rabbinic texts, prostitutes and children speak the truth; children have the mouths of babes, a common trope in many literatures, and prostitutes are the unusual example of a completely free social class—women who create their own incomes and sexual identities, unburdened by and even in control of the men around them. To demonstrate that the encounter with the *pardes* has rendered him fundamentally changed, Elisha once again commits an act of violence to the fertile soil of the *pardes* by uprooting a radish. The prostitute then speaks the truth: he cannot be that one; he must be another. This etiology of the name that Elisha acquires after his fall also reveals the sad truth of masking and naming, in that Elisha has not only fallen in his own estimation—after all, one of the sadnesses of post-Enlightenment Jewishness and religion in general is the low estimation in which we hold ourselves as committed spiritual beings—but even in the eyes of the socially marginal. Even to the unnamed prostitute, to be Rabbi Elisha ben Avuyah was something to behold; this coarseness that has become him, this explicit violation of both sexual norms and religious-behavioral names, does not suit a person of his station. Elisha's own dissonance, based on what he sees, creates an equally powerful dissonance in those who see him, a dissonance that in turns eliminates the true Elisha from public view. You are not Elisha, says she, for Elisha would not behave this way; you must be *another*.

Elisha's life in this Talmudic narrative then becomes expressed, as befits a sage (even a fallen one), in a series of coded philosophical dialogues. His interlocutor, Rabbi Meir, is both a fellow student of Akiva's and clearly a student of Elisha's as well; Elisha initiates the dialogues and corrects the wrong interpretations offered by Meir. This imbalance and the attending visual image of *Aher* on the horse and Meir following, absorbing his Torah all the while, are astonishing. Besides its merits for portraying a world of Jewish pluralism that values Torah over the aesthetics of choices and appearances (and it is important that we tell that story!), the narrative reinforces the undercurrent of Elisha's inability to get away from his past, the sense that sageship is still in his blood. Torah and wisdom have fixed canons, but their force derives from their ability to become still, small voices in our own hearts and minds. This is personal to Elisha; he engages in a certain *hesed* in perpetuating the Torah of others even if he cannot find his way back in, even if he feels the door to the Law is closed to him.

These dialogues frustrate Rabbi Meir. If Elisha's learning inclines him to believe that the Torah allows for him to repent from his ways, why will he not heed his own words? Elisha continues to hear the words spoken perhaps only to him, "beyond the curtain" where the wizard sits, that he alone may not come back. The notion that he would be "fixed"—that a simple *takanah*, or repair, could remedy this loss—misses the essence of what Elisha cannot do. Perhaps he might be fixed; can he ever be restored? Each of the dialogues builds up Meir's frustration, as the rabbis ceaselessly contrast Meir's legality and sense of order, his insistence on right answers, against the ambiguous duality modeled by Elisha's teaching. Rather surprisingly, Elisha retains the upper hand, aided by his stronger ability to marshal on his side the legacy of Rabbi Akiva that they both share. Dissonance and ambiguity triumph over singularity and clarity in this story as the inheritors of Torah, much to the consternation both of Rabbi Meir and many classical commentators forced to reckon with a story much more sympathetic to the whims of change than these commentators might be.

Even in the violent and troubling account that ensues, in the drama of study house after study house wherein Elisha hears nothing but what Rabbi Bradley Artson calls "a Torah of hate," a vicious series of voices directed at him, the text stops short of condemning Elisha and justifying his place outside the pantheon of Torah sages. The metaphor of a child cut into pieces evokes the concubine of Gibeah from the nineteenth chapter of the Book of Judges, whose woebegone fate bespeaks not her own iniquity but the failure and corruption of the entire society around her. Though Elisha may wield the knife, he is the victim in this story; the metaphorical violence with which he is associated here means to elevate him to the role of prophet, the single individual around whom a corrupt system fails to integrate the dissonant, fails to respond to the legitimacy of his critique, insists on making him alien to the community of Israel. If our communities cannot sustain, tolerate, absorb, and even continue to elevate those in our midst who are afflicted and confused, those who will seek and seek even to the point of unsettling discovery—then our communities are as wretched as that of Gibeah.

Finally, Elisha dies, and this extended parable hinges ultimately on what happens next. After Elisha's death, the stakes are actually higher—just as we do not fully judge anyone or anything until it becomes part of our memory, and just as we judge consciously and unconsciously alike. A legacy, after all, is nothing but the continuous choices that the survivors make about the memory of the departed. People, ideas, and events live or die in our memories, as we attempt to survive those whom we must leave behind and hold on to those whose lives are important to our surviving.

The rabbis are conflicted about Elisha, and the metaphor they choose to play out this ambivalence is magnificent. The rabbis imagine Elisha hanging in purgatory, neither condemned to hell nor ascending to heaven. Do rabbis control the actual outcome of the dead?? Rather subversively, I think, the rabbis are suggesting that how we remember the deceased mirrors, if not implicitly determines, what their afterlife looks like. In the rabbinic understanding of the afterlife, everyone ultimately ascends to heaven; it is just that the sinners must bide some time in the other place before being allowed to enter the world to come. In Elisha's case, it is not altogether clear to which place he is destined and where he belongs. Fittingly, the dissonance of his own mind yields a parallel dissonance of memory. Does his wisdom and scholarship buy him a pass for his transgressions? Or put differently: do we exempt him from punishment because we actually identify and sympathize with his struggle?

Rabbi Meir the literalist takes a predictably hard line, embodying in this story one half of the polar and dissonant divine attributes, that of judgment and stricture. He demands that Elisha bide his time with the sinners, and pledges to make it so. Perhaps the way to understand his threat—"when I die"—is to see Rabbi Meir as the inheritor of Elisha's legacy, the executor of his memory. As long as

Rabbi Meir lived, his students would know the real Elisha: not totally villainous, but insufficiently a victim to merit the benefit of the doubt. Meir outlives Elisha, and with the merit of that stroke of luck stands in control of how we remember his teacher. The smoke rises from Elisha's grave as he burns in hell.

Rabbi Yochanan, however, embodies the twin attribute to justice, that of *rahamim*: compassion manifest in an act of deep love and generosity, a full depiction of love as the practice of seeking. Is it a great accomplishment to stand in judgment of those who come before us, to so quickly judge and jettison the challenges that their nuances and complexities lodge in our minds? Is willful amnesia really a cure for the provocation of the past, and shouldn't we instead heed its implications for our betterment? What's more, Rabbi Yochanan goes on to say, the punishment intended for Elisha is better applied to his custodians—to all of us who allowed him to falter in our midst. A stronger self-indictment cannot be found in all of rabbinic literature, and this message deserves to be posted in all educational environments, in every classroom: when our students fail in the face of real and meaningful challenges, their failure is on us. We may not be able to protect them from dissonance, and in fact we do not want to. We may not want to shield them from that struggle. But what we owe them in those moments is compassion, love, mercy, and the willingness to let their struggles be validated by the reality of similar struggles by others greater and ostensibly more pious than they are. Elisha belongs in our memory as a reminder of our humanity and our complexity, as a paradigm of every existential struggle that Jews have faced and will face in the wake of a changing lived reality. Rabbi Yochanan saves Elisha and saves his memory, descending to hell and, as with a child, taking him by the hand and escorting him upward. Elisha's good name is restored, for that is how we are instructed to remember him.

Who then are these rabbis? They may be historical figures, but there is little utility in thinking of the parable of Elisha as a historical text; the characters are literary figures, but this is more than a story. They are also archetypes, similar to the way in which the four sons function in the Passover Haggadah as means to stimulate a discussion on pedagogy. In the Haggadah, the same narrative of Exodus is narrated to all four children—albeit differently based on their respective needs, interests, and capabilities. Here stand these four paradigms back in the Garden of Enlightenment, and perhaps they never left, and perhaps this happens every few thousand years. There are the fundamentalists, those to whom enlightenment is to be feared; maybe rightly, but with social consequences we may find to be unpalatable. Elsewhere in the Talmud, Akiva is described as being tempted by a ne'er-do-well antagonist with the company of two well-oiled young maidens; Akiva does not merely resist their advances, he claims that they reek to him of carrion. For some Jews, the fear and stench of modernity is so strong that they live lives apart. There is something of valor in this, maybe, and something that in and of itself feels deeply lost.

Then there are the Jews of ben Zoma and ben Azzai—those crippled by modernity to either near-alienation or total loss. This is perhaps the place at which the rabbinic narrative departs most dramatically from the contemporary history we now seem to be writing. The rabbis do something interesting here to these two men: with some sadness and regret, they end their story. In the modern experience, it is in these two rabbis that the Jewish community would invest the most time, energy, and anxiety—on those who are either lost or on the liminal edge of the community. Read not "affected," read "assimilated"—and lo, ben Zoma's fixation on seeing, the seduction of what he sees, makes him constitutionally unable or uninterested in reentering the community of Israel. But the rabbis let ben Zoma go, and barely even mourn ben Azzai. At the juncture of enlightenment, in the confrontation with the revelatory, there are costs and casualties. Our community fixates on and invests enormous resources in those most on the outside, hardly even looking in. Are resources best utilized on the wounded and disinterested?

And then there is Elisha. It is amazing that this text hinges primarily on Elisha's experience. As anomalous as Elisha is in the rabbinic corpus, as the rabbi who got away, this text seems to embrace Elisha as the most relatable, most immanent, and most paradigmatic. Other narratives elsewhere in the rabbinic corpus help us understand why. In one text parallel to ours, the Jerusalem Talmud's version of these events, Elisha is described as witnessing a child fall from a tree to his death after being dispatched by his father to shoo away the mother-bird and take the eggs. In that one act, the child has properly fulfilled the two biblical commandments that explicitly promise long life for their proper performance—honoring one's father and mother, and sending away the mother bird before taking the young. The child's death evokes the same cognitive dissonance for Elisha that we saw in our core text, but in a most recognizable and hopeless theological frame: How can such a punishment befall the righteous in the performance of the good deed? How can bad things happen to good people? Or, in another rabbinic version, Elisha witnesses the horrifying—but to twentieth century eyes, strangely familiar—sight of the tongue of a mellifluous sage dragged through the dirt by a stray dog after the rabbi's torturous death and disfigurement. Elisha expresses the altogether human skepticism, or call it holy fear, of the imbalance between piety and its supposed rewards. Is this what the righteous deserve? Elisha is not the only sage in the rabbinic corpus to stand horrified at God's "justice" in the face of evil; elsewhere, in a separate text, the rabbis place the identical words that Elisha utters—"Is this Torah, and is this its reward?"—in the mouth of none other than Moses as he watches the skin flayed off of our Rabbi Akiva. God's answer—Silence! That is how I have decreed!—is as shallow to Moses as it is to Elisha, as it is an answer completely incapable of matching the force of the question. This answer requires a paradigm of faith rooted in luck, enviable conviction, or suppression of our instinctual responses. Elisha's dissonance, whether brought about by the problem of theodicy specifically or in the face of the larger theological and existential gymnastics that he faces in the world of "enlightenment," is altogether understandable to the rabbis. More than Akiva, more than ben Zoma and ben Azzai, Elisha's story is the one the rabbis know too well, and a story they understand too personally.

No doubt, the rabbis regret Elisha's choices and how he responds to his dissonance. They would sooner have him in the study house with Meir, not violating the Sabbath on a horse or in the orchard, not consorting with prostitutes, and known by his real name with which he is remembered in other rabbinic texts for his erudition rather than this demeaning sobriquet. They want him to do something that perhaps they can do, or that perhaps they cannot. After all, his experience is quite different from theirs. Did they ever actually enter the orchard, or do they only recall the story of when he did? They want him to do the impossible: to inhabit the dissonance, to see before him what threatens to undermine the stable ground on which he stands and yet still to obey the laws of that ground. Most of all, they are desperate for him to come back—la'shuv. This is the hardest challenge of the postcritical moment. It feels like a mandate to turn back the clock, to unsee, to pretend, to assume a "second naivete." No wonder Elisha hears the echoing prohibition against his return: that door seems hopelessly closed to him, if not totally uninteresting.

But teshuva—restoration—is at its core a postcritical act, and one that should not require us to make untenable choices. The ultimate act of repentance is the ability to inhabit an identical scenario in which a transgression occurred, and to make a different choice. Returning does not involve reversing one's actions, or pretending they did not happen; it is not an evolutionary regression, but rather a wildly progressive worldview. A person who can truly return and change direction has so obviously exceeded the merits of someone who has never been challenged. The rabbis seem so desperate for Elisha to follow this path, and they become locked with Elisha in an unwinnable fight: to them, the door back in is wide open. To him, the door is blocked—as is the Garden of Eden—by swords preventing his entry.

The only remaining route of return for Elisha is through how he is remembered. How we tell our stories is the process by which we own the past and, in turn, the means by which we chart the future with confidence and authenticity. The rabbis not only end their story with a saved Elisha, they implicitly tell us that their story and our story are best routed through him. Ben Zoma and ben Azzai are gone, Rabbi Akiva is inaccessible, but Elisha is most closely us—occupying a place of dissonance, struggling with his choices, making those around him struggle with their choices, and ultimately departing and making us feel conflicted as to whether his struggles were his own or ours, whether he failed us, we failed him, or whether no one failed at all. The story becomes one of a loss of commanded-ness, seeing and its consequences, of love and its sacrifices, and ultimately of return and restoration: not in Elisha's lifetime, but in how we narrate his story.

# ...and Back Again

## WHAT WILL BE the FUTURE of the JEWISH PAST?

> But the man and the age are rare who can choose
> their own path; we have generally only a choice
> between going ahead in the direction already chosen,
> or halting and blocking the path for others. The only
> kind of reform usually possible is reform from within:
> a more intimate study and more intelligent use of the
> traditional forms. Disaster follows rebellion against
> tradition or against utility, which are the basis and
> root of our taste and progress. But, within the given
> school, and as exponents of its spirit, we can adapt
> and perfect our works, if haply we are better inspired
> than our predecessors.
> —*George Santayana*, The Sense of Beauty

Recently the *New York Times* reported on the famous shtetl photographs taken and published by Roman Vishniac. The journalist Alana Newhouse had dug up the records at Vishniac's daughter's home and those of the organization that had dispatched him as a documentarian, and discovered that the mythic undercurrent of the photos themselves and especially the captions was "false": Vishniac had crafted a particular narrative around and about the photos, sometimes placing together images that had no connection in real life, in order to amplify the pathos and a particular understanding of the shtetl culture. He had been wildly successful, even if (or perhaps because) it was not widely known that he had been dispatched by a Jewish organization hoping to use the photos in a fundraising campaign, and even if the traditionalist-impoverished picture that his lens painted of the shtetl was a historical misrepresentation of a far more complex phenomenon.

The Vishniac photos then are the bear/log that we encountered earlier, and the intense response generated by the article showed that a particularly sensitive nerve had been touched. Vishniac's photos had been deeply inspirational and evocative to multiple generations of Jews—it was the frightening bear, one that had conveyed a stable impression of the "vanished world" from before the Holocaust. Indeed, this awe-inspiring collection implicitly told a story about how to interpret the magnitude of the loss involved in the Holocaust, the sense of fear, and the piety of the past. And this story was accentuated in the increased publication and editing of the book over time and its juxtaposition with the voice of Elie Wiesel as the author of the book's foreword. Like a revelatory experience, the Vishniac images became canonized in their own unique way; and like the scientists, empiricists, and historians, the author of this article sought to question that canonization.

So here, photographs jog the memories of those who see them, and make for what—distorted memory? Selective memory? And when the photos are demystified, what becomes of the identity that has been generated around them, the story that binds past and present? We do have to prepare ourselves for demystification even of the highly unmystical, like photos from a shtetl. Jewish memory-making has subsisted in our ability to take historical moments, events, episodes—regardless of how sublime or mundane—and make them mythically instructive. Leon Wieseltier is quoted at the end of Newhouse's article as follows:

Jews should be absolutely elated—and not at all surprised—to discover that Jewish life in Poland was like human society anywhere, in that it contained all the human types and all of the human experiences. Will they resent being deprived by the full historical record of the holy beards and the mystical sparks, or will they have the wisdom to say, "Good, they were blessedly like all of us"?

For historians, the desire to see generative and restorative myth based on our past hold us together does not mean we turn our back on the historical project of establishing empirical truth when we can and demystifying what should be human and mundane. But we must be conscious of the costs, and eager to resupply the mythology as needed. A mythology on shtetl *normalcy* is just fine! It may supply what this generation of Jews needs more aptly, and more accurately, than what previous generations needed. But we should not mistake accuracy for truth—for both the old myths and new myths expressed something true and deep for their stakeholders—nor should we mistake our historical consciousness for a sense of having outgrown or left behind sacred myth and the purposefulness it carries.

This sense that time is slipping away, that the commanding past is becoming more elusive, has been a key concern and a recurring theme in modern Jewish thought. I wonder whether this is one of the messages of Kafka's parable "Before the Law":

Before the law sits a gatekeeper. To this gatekeeper comes a man from the country who asks to gain entry into the law. But the gatekeeper says that he cannot grant him entry at the moment. The man thinks about it and then asks if he will be allowed to come in later on. "It is possible," says the gatekeeper, "but not now." At the moment the gate to the law stands open, as always, and the gatekeeper walks to the side, so the man bends over in order to see through the gate into the inside. When the gatekeeper notices that, he laughs and says: "If it tempts you so much, try it in spite of my prohibition. But take note: I am powerful. And I am only the most lowly gatekeeper. But from room to room stand gatekeepers, each more powerful than the other. I can't endure even one glimpse of the third." The man from the country has not expected such difficulties: the law should always be accessible for everyone, he thinks, but as he now looks more closely at the gatekeeper in his fur coat, at his large pointed nose and his long, thin, black Tartar's beard, he decides that it would be better to wait until he gets permission to go inside. The gatekeeper gives him a stool and allows him to sit down at the side in front of the gate. There he sits for days and years. He makes many attempts to be let in, and he wears the gatekeeper out with his requests. The gatekeeper often interrogates him briefly, questioning him about his homeland and many other things, but they are indifferent questions, the kind great men put, and at the end he always tells him once more that he cannot let him inside yet. The man, who has equipped himself with many things for his journey, spends everything, no matter how valuable, to win over the gatekeeper. The latter takes it all but, as he does so, says, "I am taking this only so that you do not think you have failed to do anything." During the many years the man observes the gatekeeper almost continuously. He forgets the other gatekeepers, and this one seems to him the only obstacle for entry into the law. He curses the unlucky circumstance, in the first years thoughtlessly and out loud, later, as he grows old, he still mumbles to himself. He becomes childish and, since in the long years studying the gatekeeper he has come to know the fleas in his fur collar, he even asks the fleas to help him persuade the gatekeeper. Finally his eyesight grows weak, and he does not know whether things are really darker around him or whether his eyes are merely deceiving him. But he recognizes now in the darkness an illumination which breaks inextinguishably out of the gateway to the law. Now he no longer has much time to live. Before his death he gathers in his head all his experiences of the entire time up into one question which he has not yet put to the gatekeeper. He waves to him, since he can no longer lift up his stiffening body. The gatekeeper has to bend way down to him, for the great difference has changed things to the disadvantage of the man. "What do you still want to know, then?" asks the gatekeeper. "You are insatiable." "Everyone strives after the law," says the man, "so how is it that in these many years no one except me has requested entry?" The gatekeeper sees that the man is already dying and, in order to reach his diminishing sense of hearing, he shouts at him, "Here no one else can gain entry, since this entrance was assigned only to you. I'm going now to close it."

In various interpretations this parable refers to the basic absurdity of modern life, or speaks to the challenge of individualism in an age of empire, and so on. But there is also a Days of Awe–like urgency in this parable that amplifies the sense of urgency needed in human behavior and in human initiative, as our world seems to drift past us. When Arnie Eisen and Steven M. Cohen talk about the emergence of the "sovereign self" in contemporary Jewish life and the turn inward from the communal sphere to the personal sphere in search of meaning, they introduce a new sociological reality but also an enormous ideological and philosophical challenge that is actually rebuked by Kafka's narrative. The notion that each individual has a door or gateway to the law reinforces the idea that our paths in this world are individuated, but at the same time suggests that what lies on the other side is a collective treasure, and that these hallways lead to the same pot of gold. If the Jewish sovereign self triumphs not only in how each individual searches, but also in what outcomes he finds, it is hard to imagine the success of the collective experience. Of course, we do not want to hinge Jewish collectivism on identical shared outcomes, for we fear reducing the collective experience to some lowest common denominator. For this reason, perhaps the more useful understanding of "the law" is a shared mobilization and understanding of what some have called a "usable past." Our individualized, pluralistic, and meaningfully different routes toward relevant Jewishness hinge on the ability to functionally hold together; perhaps less in seeking a specific set of common outcomes and more in stemming from a shared set of common heritages.

The context of classical Jewish communal prayer offers a comparable example. Rabbi Joseph B. Soloveitchik differentiates between the experience of praying as an individual within a communal context, and the prayer of the community as articulated aloud by the prayer leader—what he calls the *tefillat ha-tzibur*, the prayer of the community. The immediate concern is the legal obligations that befall an individual during this moment of communal prayer, but for our purposes we should consider the phenomenological differences between when an individual prays as part of a community and when an individual shares in the prayer of the community. The silent prayer of the individual is the idealized context for the emergence of the sovereign self: in classical Jewish prayer, the prayer is silent and personal. For some, a fixed liturgy is freeing, for some alienating; and the context of silence or at least hushed tones can allow the prayer to take on its deeply personalized intonations. It can be a prayer of formulae or of beseeching, hovering in the balance between fixedness and fluidity. In the prayer of the community, however, the sovereign self is subordinated to the collective language and intonation selected by the prayer leader and affirmed in the prayer book. An individual must find, in this latter model, a route from within the fixedness to find his or her own voice, to hear his or her own needs articulated in the fixed language. This experience of the individual, hovering between the sovereign self and belonging to a collective, is one of productive tension. In drawing a parable to the argument in this book, the prayer of the collective is comparable to what we make of our past. Without sublimating or silencing the plaintive, penitent, and pleading voice of the individual petitioner, there is still a place for a collective voice articulating a shared vision in shared language and predicated on a shared narrative. There is not only a place for this voice, but there is a strength that the individuated experience cannot command on its own.

Jewish cultural expression, which in turn forms Jewish ideology, has been remarkably able to thread together the old and the new in such a way that feels authentic to the old while completely consonant with the new. In the words of Gerson Cohen, "In each and every generation we have had our exegetes, and we speak proudly of *dor dor vedorshav*, who have been able to take a core, reinterpret it and maintain its authenticity through *change* and thereby through *contemporary relevance*." Or, as David Hartman shows in the writings of Rabbi Soloveitchik, both receptivity and creativity (or, more accurately, innovation) intertwine in halakhic Judaism, and this union forms a central feature of what it is to live within a confined system. It is extremely surprising to the outsider to traditional and halakhic Judaism that this closed and internal tradition speaks so frequently about the forces of creativity and change.

Still, at the core of Jewish expression is innovation. Innovation, as opposed to creation and creativity, entails the assertion of the new in the framework or with the language of the old. In the opening of the Midrash Rabbah, the classical rabbis' earliest collection of commentaries on Genesis, the rabbis struggle with the absolute nature of the creation, and attenuate its force considerably. Their interpretations give nuance to the absolute creative force, and instead imagine that God created the world with a blueprint in hand, and that certain aspects of the known world actually preceded the creation of the universe. The biblical scholar Jon Levenson shows how the Bible itself rejects the notion of creation ex nihilo, and that reading Genesis together with Psalms and other biblical texts reveals that creation comes about based on a divine triumph over existing elements. Even the majesty of creation is merely the improving on existing forms.

Is this innovative interpreting a disappearing art? The extremes of Jewish behavior both reject this nuanced stance, either militantly denying the legitimacy of innovation in favor of ungainly and bloated veneration of the old, or rejecting the utility of classical forms in reverence to the untested new. The venerable, vulnerable, and contested middle ground struggles with the mechanics of balancing on this threshold, with little more than Potter Stewart–like logic—we know authenticity when we see it—to discern when change has gone too far or when the ancient feels antiquated.

A revitalized notion of return would seek to return us to exactly this middle place: not to a different time or place in Jewish consciousness, but to the in-betweenness, the liminality, of living on the literal cutting edge—at the intersection between the overwhelming knowledge of past paradigms and the first tingling sense of being owned by the past, and the still-tantalizing sense that we are better served by what has yet to come. Something is aflutter in contemporary Jewish life, a combination of an awareness of the chasm that appears between us and our past—like Wile E. Coyote sensing for the first time that he is off the cliff—and a craving for the stability of having our feet back on solid ground. The Kafka text reminds us that to live in this moment is itself to occupy familiar ground, that these moments of awareness of loss, of building toward stability, have occupied the Jewish imagination in the past, even if they failed then to find permanent resonance. When we witness a revitalization of Jewish engagement with text as a means of both engagement and personal transformation, we are reminded of Franz Rosenzweig, articulating a similar moment to the one in which we live now, a moment that tragically neither he nor German Jewry could live to see fulfilled:

> It could hardly be asserted that the great urgency of the present moment is to organize the science of Judaism or to prompt both Jews and non-Jews to the endless writings of books on Jewish subjects. Books are not now the prime need of the day. But what we need more than ever, or at least as much as ever, are human beings—Jewish human beings, to use a catchword that should be cleansed of the partisan associations still clinging to it.

The big idea of this book—hopefully not the kind of book that Rosenzweig laments—is that the next stage for the Jewish future lies in our ability to connect deeply with our past. When we talk about our past, we mean more than the specific events of history; we mean the ideological frameworks developed in classical Jewish thought that enabled the absorbing of the changing world into ongoing definitions of Jewishness. I have argued that the core categories of Jewish thought and behavior, as encapsulated in the key terms for each chapter, are flexible enough to connect to the contemporary Jewish experience; and that meaningful Jewish continuity, the bridge between our powerful past and our uncertain future, lies in our ability to connect with these core categories. I have also suggested here that we heed Rosenzweig's call to focus less on the rigorous documenting of Jews and Jewishness—manifest in our constant archiving of our past, and counting of our people—and spend more time investing in the humanity in our stories that echoes in our souls.

This suggestion means we are capable of both appreciating and going beyond the archetypal narratives of the Jewish past that meant so much to Jewish cultural survival. Jewish memory literature in the past was characterized by the routing of contemporary experiences into the master interpretive structures, so that experiences that appeared new—and, in some cases, incomprehensible—became theologically and culturally familiar. In this book, I have both modeled this approach and extended it beyond its role in helping Jews weather crisis and toward a broader system of finding our place as both we and the world around us evolve. We must go further, though, in recognizing the ways in which the narratives themselves also must change, as they reflect the ways we are growing as storytellers. The modern Jewish experience is too marvelously complex to be distilled into archetypes; any archetypes must merely be the vehicles for systematic growth and change.

In a previous chapter we looked at *ahavah* and explored the centrality of love to our lives as Jews. Left out of this discussion was the full version of one of the most famous rabbinic teachings about love, which reads as follows:

> *And you shall love your neighbor as yourself*: Rabbi Akiva says, "This is a great principle of Torah." Ben Azzai says, "*This is the book of generations of mankind*"—this is an even greater principle.

Rabbi Akiva's teaching is well known and in some ways obvious. We understand how loving one's neighbor can create not just the basis of civil society but also the very fabric of the Torah. Generosity and civic-mindedness that go beyond politeness to achieve the power of a commanded principle can engender human receptiveness to the broader scope of commitment and human responsibility. But ben Azzai? How does this generic phrase of Genesis achieve the same power? Ben Azzai cites a verse from the beginning of the fifth chapter of Genesis, after the culmination of the drama between Cain and Abel and prior to the first chronicling of fathers-and-sons, a phrase that subsequently recurs as an intermezzo to the narratives of the book in summarizing the various generations of parents and children.

One possible reading would link the two teachings, and suggest that both Akiva and ben Azzai are speaking about the centrality of fellowship in the message of the Torah—but whereas Akiva speaks only about particularism, about fellowship to our neighbors and those to whom we are already linked, ben Azzai routes human responsibility all the way back to the creation of humankind. Ben Azzai then constitutes a universalistic response to Akiva.

But I would suggest that something else lies in ben Azzai's teaching that resonates with the message of this book. The verse reads, "This is the book of the generations of mankind," or perhaps "the generations of Adam," or even "the stories of Adam." Our stories make up our generations, by segmenting an otherwise inseparable human narrative. Is ben Azzai suggesting that in our stories about our world we create the possibility for the instantiation of Torah, for the penetration of our values—that as we narrate the world, we make Torah possible? Perhaps ben Azzai responds to the equivocating and neutralizing message of Rabbi Akiva and its horizontal message—we are defined by how we act toward those around us— by insisting that there is something vertical to be said as well, that we are also defined in our essence by where we come from, by who precedes us, and by who sets forth to succeed us. Without the markers of past, present, and future, Jewishness evolves immeasurably; it is difficult to keep it in relationship to the benchmark of Torah. The Talmud leaves these two positions standing and unresolved, possibly because one cannot definitively establish which one of these ideas is more "core" than the other, but also possibly because it realizes that Jews must live on both axes: in a community of peers, who keep us conscious of our moment at the top of history; and in relationship to our past, which keeps us conscious of our responsibilities embedded in our memory.

In the discussion of memory and mitzvah, we looked at a few key rabbinic texts that talked about tinokot, or children; and in the parable, we saw the way the rabbis again placed wisdom in the mouths of children, echoing and interpreting the biblical phrase "From the mouths of babes . . ." (Psalms 8:2). Elsewhere the rabbis amplify this message, teaching that the world only exists based on the merits of the whisperings and murmurings of children—tinokot—in the schoolhouses of their teachers. But the rabbis also make reference to these tinokot in one critical context, in mocking the way the children of Israel fled Mount Sinai after the revelation and the giving of the Torah. The rabbis pick up on the terminology in the biblical text, which quickly ends the story of the revelation by describing the departure of the Israelites and their journey away, to suggest that the children of Israel left Sinai "like children fleeing a school-house." A familiar polemic leveled against children in educational environments around summertime, the invective is true to our image of the last day of elementary school, the sense that we are unbound from our obligations to learn and even remember what we have learned for long stretches of time. This is a lament to the rabbis, that this culture even pervades the children of Israel in the aftermath of the transformative moment of Sinai—that even after witnessing the sound and the fury, even after having their eyes opened in revelatory marvel, even after having accepted the yoke of commandment and responsibility, they still instinctively fled the scene, as though no longer being there would release them from their sworn commitments.

Of course, the rabbis here are mocking that flight to remind us that our commitments and covenants are equally binding—whether we stand at the foot of Sinai or flee from its environs. I wonder sometimes whether the Jewish experience of modernity, sometimes characterized as the unfettering of Jewish political and intellectual constraints, is more evocative of this caricature of the Jewish people at the end of the Sinai revelation: the darkened sky, silence restored, and the momentary instinct to bolt from all that we have taken on during the flashes of glory. And some of the attempts we make to correct that historical error mistake memorialization for memory, as though we would remedy this historical figure by building merely a museum to Mount Sinai. Memory has to have a rhythm and cadence that monuments alone can never achieve.

I began this book with one of the paradoxes of modern Jewish life: we know now, as a collective, more about the past than Jews ever have before and more accurately, but collectively we lack for a deep relationship with the same past. Our knowledge of the past has created distance from it. In the subsequent chapters, I outlined a system by which we might not only become reacquainted with our Jewish selves but with how we might appreciate even a past laden with complexities. Let me now end with a second troublesome paradox. The greatest legacy of the Enlightenment for Jews and modern Judaism has been widespread ignorance of the core elements of Jewishness, and the apparent sensibility that knowledge is not a prerequisite for Jewishness except for people who are trying to make their way in.

I think that I have made the case that one source of this problem has been the mistaken sensibility that we are unable to reconcile the dissonance between the axioms of Torah and tradition and the prying eyes of empiricism and evolution. I have suggested that we certainly can see the world and all its complexity, understand our history with its true triumphs and failings, seek knowledge and understanding, and still return rehabilitated to our core identity.

So in the section on mitzvah, we explored the deep ways in which memory and commandedness are bound up with each other—that when we remember who we are, we also remember our commitments. In discussing yir'ah, we saw that seeing is not the same as believing; that in fact we cannot rely overmuch on our sight to create our dependencies, that seeing the revelation cannot be the only experience that ties us to its implications. Skepticism need not exonerate us from our responsibilities. In examining ahavah, we considered what is involved with building a covenantal relationship with that for which we aspire: how love represents an act of our seeking out what we want to become, the learning and craving of learning that make us whole. In considering how hurban has functioned in the Jewish past, we considered how we might stitch over—or perhaps even find ways to tolerate—the rupture in Jewish life wrought by the events of the past century. And teshuva is the system by which we progress in seeking restoration of our whole selves, by which we re-place ourselves in the moments in time and in consciousness and live them again—better, newer, more fully.

Can the Jewish people go back to Sinai—or better, can we reimagine what it would be to walk away again whole from Mount Sinai rather than fleeing in fear from its orbit of commitments? Memory does not entail a wholesale return to Sinai, an overvalorization of a hot day in a remote desert with a lousy sense of direction. It means a restoring of the core values, commitments, and obligations—as articulated by our tradition, in compelling but sometimes-inaccessible language—in order to proceed, whole, into the future. I hope we are confident enough to do so.

# Postscript

JEWS HAVE SIX SENSES
Touch, taste, sight, smell, hearing . . . memory.
While Gentiles experience and process the world
through the traditional senses, and use memory only
as a second-order means of interpreting events, for
Jews memory is no less primary than the prick of a
pin, or its silver glimmer, or the taste of the blood
it pulls from the finger. The Jew is pricked by a pin
and remembers other pins. It is only by tracing the
pinprick back to other pinpricks—when his mother
tried to fix his sleeve while his arm was still in it, when
his grandfather's fingers fell asleep while stroking his
great-grandfather's damp forehead, when Abraham
tested the knife point to be sure Isaac would feel no
pain—that the Jew is able to know why it hurts.

When a Jew encounters a pin, he asks: *What does it
remember like?*
—*Jonathan Safran Foer,*
Everything Is Illuminated

147

My goal in writing this book has been to introduce a system and a conceptual framework to think about the Jewishness of our time. The reader may understandably now be asking: to what does this translate? What are the programmatic and specific takeaways that model this approach to Jewish memory, or that seek to put Jewish memory back in place? I am resistant to this question because I believe that it stems from a basic assumption in the contemporary organized Jewish community, that serious problems always require programmatic solutions. A philosophical approach thinks more about the conceptual background to the problem, and helps us condition our thinking about it.

One of my high school teachers likened the role of the educator to the process of straightening a bent tree. The best way to get it straight would be to bend it all the way in the other direction. Simply pushing it upright would not work. This is conceivably true, and I think it accurately describes how we as a community provide programmatic solutions to problems. When they are smaller problems, reflective of a mere wayward tilt, there is no reason this technique should not work. But over time, as a constantly bent plant pushed back and forth will eventually snap, our programmatic attempts to shift and reorient our communities may have deleterious long-term effects, either destabilizing us in our search for real meaning or even building up a plaque around the base of our tree that misleads us to believe it is really standing straight. Here is a provocative example: it is a widely observed phenomenon in the North American Jewish community that the visceral relationship that an older generation of Jews felt toward the state of Israel and its people has not fully passed on to the younger generation. Although a vigorous debate surrounds the sources of this problem and its manifestations, sociological data bears out the problem's rough outline. The programmatic solutions seek to correct the flaw: we can bend the tree by sending thousands of young people to Israel, by bringing Israel to campus, by flooding our educational environments with new Israel messaging. But these programmatic solutions—which may be effective in the short term—do not take seriously the problem itself, which is rooted in how we change over time, how we tell stories from one generation to the next, how our values evolve in relationship to our evolving realities. If we correct this astigmatic moment in the sphere of Jewish peoplehood with a specific program agenda, what blind spots are we creating in the process for the next generation to fixate on anxiously?

In this book I have argued both explicitly and implicitly that the classical rabbis approached a moment of crisis that is conceptually similar to the challenges of modernity. The rabbis faced challenges of evolving political and corporate identity, of new intellectual, philosophical, and aesthetic realities that the tradition was often too traditional to confront, and a geographically diversifying and polarizing community that lacked for implicit global identity. To deal with these challenges the rabbis created both programmatic solutions, the elements of classical Jewish life and practice that became the hallmarks of rabbinic culture, as well as a philosophical approach to the passage of time and to the instantiation of change.

As such, if we must end with some programmatic thinking, I would turn again to the rabbis for their wisdom, and one of their aphorisms that tells us what lies at the core of the rabbinic enterprise:

> Mishnah Peah, 1:1
>
> These are the matters that have no fixed quantity. . . . And these are the matters from which a person derives benefit in this world, and the principal remains in the coming world: Honoring one's father and mother; acts of lovingkindness; and making peace between a man and his fellow. And the study of Torah correlates to all three.

The rabbis here describe two anomalous categories of commandments—first, a list of obligations that can be fulfilled without regard for quantity, either a lower limit or an upper limit. The commandment to perform acts of lovingkindness is ongoing and limitless, so we get "credit," so to speak, for the small acts, but at the same time we never exhaust our responsibility to keep doing them. This is a double-edged sword, of course. On one hand, we are forever bound to these activities; on the other, rather than giving the sense that these obligations are never fulfilled, the rabbis craft a process of continual fulfillment.

The second category here is slightly more theologically complex. These mitzvot represent the behaviors that only yield a portion of their ultimate reward in this lifetime. I think we are meant to read this less as a celebration of the world to come or of redemptive theology in general, and more as a realistic recognition of what is entailed in performing the acts of commanded good behavior that are, at their core, altruistic or that yield something other than direct benefits for the actor. If I bring about reconciliation between two people, I derive some immediate benefit from this outcome—perhaps in seeing two people happier, perhaps in the self-satisfied sense of having done something good. The rabbis encourage us to take such benefits as *enough* satisfaction. The messaging of the coming world, I think, is meant to tell us that we do not always live to see the rewards for our actions, rather than that we are hedging our bets for the world to come. The pious way to read this text probably should be that we continue to act meritoriously even if the end reward is something we literally will not live to see.

This all makes sense for the three acts listed first in this category—lovingkindness, peacemaking, and respect. With all three, it is not clear what the direct return will be for the actor. Most unclear, however, is how the fourth act—the study of Torah—fits this paradigm at all. Also unclear is how we understand this word "correlates" (*k'neged*): Is the study of Torah equivalent to these acts? Does it correlate to them, or cause them? Does it correspond to them? It is a wonderfully ambiguous word that calls to mind two uses we have studied here previously, as the same word appears in God's creation of male and female—Eve is created as a helpmate *k'neged* Adam—and as Rabbi Meir uses it over and over in the hypothetical questions he poses to Elisha. The word can be relational or oppositional.

There are a number of approaches we might take in making sense of this text, and how the rabbis understand the study of Torah related to these other, ostensibly more altruistic behaviors. I am not inclined to believe that the rabbis fundamentally equate the study of Torah to helping the downtrodden or restoring harmony to places of brokenness; that would seem so shortsighted and civically untenable. Instead, perhaps we might think about this correspondence as the difference between programmatic thinking and philosophi-

cal thinking, as we just discussed. A life of Torah is the conditioning process by which we become continual change-agents capable
of navigating a changing world. Here the rabbis do not place the
study of Torah on a linear trajectory leading to positive action, as
they do in other places. Instead they imagine it as the parallel activity we undertake as we dwell amid daily challenges. Ron Heifetz and Marty Linsky introduce being on the balcony and being on
the dance floor as two equally important and symbiotic activities of
leadership. When we are on the dance floor, we are in the thick of
the activity, participating and whirling. But we cannot fully understand everything transpiring around us, not until and unless we periodically go up the staircase to the balcony to observe the action. Of
course, there too we cannot stay indefinitely, for we will miss out on
the action.

In placing Torah on this pedestal as they simultaneously introduce wholesale and idiosyncratic changes to Jewish life and practice, the rabbis implicitly remind us that these changes are not to
be idolatrously interpreted as the entirety of the rabbinic response
to crisis, or enshrined as unchanging markers of a moment when
the world changed and Judaism changed in response. That attitude
is at its core historical, and not the work of memory. No, the rabbis routed their changes to Jewish life both through generating an
ongoing mythology about themselves and their recent past, which
in turn interwove the mythology they inherited, and creating systemic change together with an ongoing mandate to meditate on the
big picture, on ideas, ethics, and values as the continual metrics by
which the world would be evaluated. In the past two decades the
Jewish community has seen a revitalized interest in the independent
value of Torah study for adults, as a practice that rehabilitates meaning as an anchor for Jewish choices. It is unfortunate when this discourse of Torah becomes routed entirely through the programmatic
model, as though this kind of learning is a counterresponse to other
Jewish behaviors, or as if the establishment must choose between
an orientation toward "meaning" and an orientation toward other
values. This is what k'neged means—a corresponding, correlating
interdependence between all our affirmative choices and all the
other activities we undertake in the world. In studying Torah we put

ourselves in a narrative as both readers and writers, recipients and transmitters. We live at the threshold of doing and acting because that is how we have been told to do and act and doing and acting because of the inclinations of our minds, hearts, and souls. And when we stay at that very threshold, when the choices we make are Jewish choices—and even if those Jewish choices differ from those made by our predecessors!—then the very world of Torah evolves for the next generation of recipients and transmitters.

Most of the other programmatic takeaways I leave for the professionals. For now, this is memory: the self-conscious act of living in vertical relationship to the past and present, and in horizontal relationship to how we thus relate to the world.

# Author's Note

I am aware that this book is unusual, that its balance between the use of scholarly categories and its concern for lived Judaism makes it anomalous to both enterprises. The book was designed to be accessible to broader audiences as compared to most academic works, and in this regard I am very much an attentive student to Yosef Hayim Yerushalmi's call at the end of *Zakhor: Jewish History and Jewish Memory*, even if this work is not one of history per se.*

In the opening chapter, I cite *Zakhor* as one of my anchoring "moments" in the broad landscape of modern Jewish memory anxiety. *Zakhor* entered an already vibrant field of memory studies and touched off a great deal of discussion. The critiques of Yerushalmi fall roughly into three categories: those who disagree entirely with his conceptual framework, those who deal less with the thesis but disagree with some of his specific historical or historiographical examples, and those who address Yerushalmi only in the context of broader discussions of historical method. Other scholarship in

*Full citations for works mentioned in this appendix can be found in the bibliography that follows.

overall agreement with Yerushalmi has tinkered with or fine-tuned his thesis, often with reference to specific historical cases. Full bibliographies and a discussion of the details of the debate are best found in David Myers's discussion of Zakhor a decade after its publication; the Yerushalmi Festschrift edited by Elisheva Carlebach, John Efron, and David Myers; and the special edition of the Jewish Quarterly Review dedicated to Zakhor on the occasion of its twenty-fifth anniversary.

As should be clear in my discussion of Zakhor, I am less interested in the historical/historiographical debate than in using Zakhor as a conceptual moment, as a peg on which modern Jewish identity hangs in a way that is productive for the broad programmatic and analytic approach in this book. In this way I am viewing Yerushalmi through the lens of the philosopher Paul Ricoeur, who emphasizes the correlation between history/historiography and secularization as features of the modern Jewish experience. Zakhor has become required reading for graduate students in Jewish history, a key piece of virtually every "methods" course. A whole generation of graduate students has matured under the austerity of its warning—be relevant while still being good! Some would argue that this conversation should continue to take place within the academic discipline of history, and I do not contest this; my argument here is that perhaps we have not fully considered the ethical and behavioral costs of staying within that discipline, and that we might consider a return to the memory model that has been left behind.

To that end, however, I do want to acknowledge that in memory, too, there are ethical implications. I believe this is implicit in the concept of false/poor memory in my discussion of Holocaust memory, and in my taking for granted that selective memory comes with serious costs, including the deep possibility of a sociopathic narcissism. But for further discussion, I recommend the reader consider Avishai Margalit's The Ethics of Memory, wherein he explores some of the ramifications that follow on the assumption of a memory consciousness.

The chapter on hurban, too, concerns a place of great scholarly and literary foment. I have attempted to summarize what I see as trends in the field, especially as they bleed into the world of Jewish public policy around memory and custody of the past, and into the public formats in which these issues are debated. I was first sensitized to this issue by reading Istvan Deak's cautionary words in the *New York Review of Books*: "An accurate record of the Holocaust has been endangered, in my opinion, by the uncritical endorsement, often by well-known Jewish writers or public figures, of virtually any survivor's account or related writings." I have learned a lot from Ruth Franklin's essays in *The New Republic* on this issue, much of which is included in her recent book, although perhaps with less polemical sharpness than the journalistic medium enabled. I also made use of Ruth Wisse's important essay in *Commentary* on the correct deployment of memory when it is made into museums, although I hesitate to draw conclusions about what political outcomes are inevitable from our choice to more programmatically "make use" of memory.

# Bibliography

Berkovits, Eliezer. *Faith after the Holocaust*. New York: Ktav, 1973.

Buber, Martin. *I and Thou*. Translated by Walter Kaufmann. New York: Touchstone, 1971.

Buber, Martin, and Nahum N. Glatzer. *On Judaism*. New York: Schocken Books, 1967.

Charme, Stuart L. "Varieties of Authenticity in Contemporary Jewish Identity." *Jewish Social Studies* 6, no. 2 (2000).

Cohen, Gerson D. "The Blessing of Assimilation in Jewish History." In *Hebrew Teachers College Commencement*. Brookline, MA, 1966.

Cohen, Steven Martin, and Arnold M. Eisen. *The Jew Within: Self, Family, and Community in America*. Bloomington: Indiana University Press, 2000.

Dan, Joseph. *The Heart and the Fountain: An Anthology of Jewish Mystical Experiences*. New York: Oxford University Press, 2002.

Deak, Istvan. "Memories of Hell." *New York Review of Books*, June 26, 1997.

Elazar, Daniel. "A Statement on Jewish Continuity." Jerusalem Center for Public Affairs, http://www.jcpa.org/dje/articles2/statement-contin.htm.

Fackenheim, Emil L. *To Mend the World: Foundations of Future Jewish Thought*. New York: Schocken Books, 1982.

Festinger, Leon. *When Prophecy Fails: A Social and Psychological Study of a Modern Group That Predicted the Destruction of the World*. New York: Harper & Row, 1956.

Foer, Jonathan Safran. *Everything Is Illuminated: A Novel.* Boston: Houghton Mifflin Co., 2002.

Franklin, Ruth. *A Thousand Darknesses: Lies and Truth in Holocaust Fiction.* Oxford: Oxford University Press, 2010.

Frey, James. *A Million Little Pieces.* New York: Random House, 2005.

Gordis, Daniel. *Saving Israel: How the Jewish People Can Win a War That May Never End.* Hoboken, NJ: John Wiley and Sons Inc., 2009.

Greenberg, Irving. "Theology after the Shoah: The Transformation of the Core Paradigm." *Modern Judaism* 26, no. 3 (2006).

Grossman, David. "Symposium on Holocaust, Storytelling, Memory, Identity: David Grossman in California; See under: Love: A Personal View." *Judaism* (Winter 2002).

Hansen, Marcus. *The Problem of the Third Generation Immigrant.* Rock Island, IL: Augustana Historical Society, 1938.

Harris, David A. "Life After." *New York Review of Books,* July 26, 2004.

Hartman, David. *Love and Terror in the God Encounter: The Theological Legacy of Rabbi Joseph B. Soloveitchik.* Woodstock, VT: Jewish Lights, 2004.

Harvey, Van Austin. *The Historian and the Believer: The Morality of Historical Knowledge and Christian Belief.* New York: Macmillan, 1966.

Heifetz, Ronald A., and Martin Linsky. *Leadership on the Line: Staying Alive through the Dangers of Leading.* Boston: Harvard Business School Press, 2002.

Heschel, Abraham Joshua. *God in Search of Man: A Philosophy of Judaism.* New York: Farrar Straus and Giroux, 1976.

Judt, Tony. *Reappraisals: Reflections on the Forgotten Twentieth Century.* New York: Penguin, 2008.

Jung, Carl. *Modern Man in Search of a Soul.* Translated by W. S. Dell and C. F. Baynes. Orlando: Harvest, 1955.

Kafka, Franz, George Steiner, Willa Muir, and Edwin Muir. *The Trial.* Definitive ed. New York: Schocken Books, 1995.

Kandel, Eric R. *In Search of Memory: The Emergence of a New Science of the Mind.* New York: Norton, 2006.

Katz, Jacob. *Tradition and Crisis: Jewish Society at the End of the Middle Ages.* Translated by Bernard Cooperman. Syracuse: Syracuse University Press, 2000.

Katz, Steven T., Shlomo Biderman, and Gershon Greenberg. *Wrestling with God: Jewish Theological Responses during and after the Holocaust.* New York: Oxford University Press, 2007.

Lansky, Aaron. *Outwitting History: The Amazing Adventures of a Man Who Rescued a Million Yiddish Books.* Chapel Hill, NC: Algonquin, 2005.

Levenson, Jon D. *Sinai and Zion: An Entry into the Jewish Bible,* New Voices in Biblical Studies. Edited by Adela Yarbro Collins and John J. Collins. New York: HarperCollins, 1987.

Liebes, Yehuda. *Studies in the Zohar*, SUNY Series in Judaica. Albany: State University of New York Press, 1993.

Lowenthal, David. *The Past Is a Foreign Country*. Cambridge: Cambridge University Press, 1999.

Margalit, Avishai. *The Ethics of Memory*. Cambridge: Harvard University Press, 2004.

Meyer, Michael. *Judaism within Modernity: Essays on Jewish History and Religion*. Detroit: Wayne State University Press, 2001.

Milgrom, Jacob. *Studies in Cultic Theology and Terminology*. Leiden, Netherlands: E. J. Brill, 1983.

Morris, Benny. *The Birth of the Palestinian Refugee Problem, 1947–1949*. New York: Cambridge University Press, 1989.

Myers, David. "Remembering Zakhor: A Super-Commentary." *History and Memory* 4, no. 2 (1992).

———. *Resisting History: Historicism and Its Discontents in German-Jewish Thought*. Princeton, NJ: Princeton University Press, 2009.

Newhouse, Alana. "A Closer Reading of Roman Vishniac." *New York Times*, April 1, 2010.

Orsi, Robert. "When 2 + 2 = 5." *The American Scholar* (Spring 2007).

Proudfoot, Wayne. *Religious Experience*. Berkeley: University of California Press, 1987.

Ricoeur, Paul. *Memory, History, Forgetting*. Chicago: University of Chicago Press, 2006.

Rosenbaum, Thane. "Remembering the Wrong Thing." *Jewish Week*, April 7, 2010.

Rosenzweig, Franz, and Nahum N. Glatzer. *On Jewish Learning*, Modern Jewish Philosophy and Religion. Madison: University of Wisconsin Press, 2002.

Sacks, Jonathan. "Creativity and Innovation in Halakha." In *Rabbinic Authority and Personal Autonomy*, edited by M. Sokol. New York: Jason Aronson, 1992.

Santayana, George, and Martin A. Coleman. *The Essential Santayana: Selected Writings*. Bloomington: Indiana University Press, 2009.

Schachter, Daniel. *Searching for Memory: The Brain, the Mind, and the Past*. New York: Basic Books, 1997.

Schachter, Jacob J. "Holocaust Commemoration and Tisha Be-Av: The Debate over Yom Ha-Shoah." *Tradition* 41, no. 2 (2008).

Schiffman, Lawrence H. *Texts and Traditions: A Source Reader for the Study of Second Temple and Rabbinic Judaism*. Hoboken, NJ: Ktav, 1997.

Scholem, Gershom. *Major Trends in Jewish Mysticism*. New York: Schocken Books Inc., 1995.

———. "Tradition and Commentary as Religious Categories in Judaism." *Studies in Comparative Religion* 3, no. 3 (1969).

Shavit, Ari. "Survival of the Fittest? An Interview with Benny Morris." *Haaretz* Friday *Magazine*, January 9, 2004.

Soloveitchik, Joseph B. "*Kol Dodi Dofek*: The Voice of My Beloved Knocks." In *Theological and Halakhic Reflections on the Holocaust*, edited by Bernhard H. Rosenberg and Fred Heuman. Hoboken, NJ: Ktav and the Rabbinical Council of America, 1992.

Stern, Eliyahu. "Realigning Jewish Peoplehood." *First Things*, February 11, 2008.

Strauss, Leo. *Spinoza's Critique of Religion*. New York: Schocken Books, 1965.

Wallach, Yona. "Tefillin." *Iton 77* (1982).

Wiesel, Elie. "Hope, Despair, and Memory." Transcript of Nobel laureate lecture,1986.

Wisse, Ruth. "How Not to Remember and How Not to Forget." *Commentary* (January 2008).

Yerushalmi, Yosef Hayim. *Zakhor: Jewish History and Jewish Memory*. Seattle: University of Washington Press, 1982.

# Index

Second Temple compared to, 84, 86; ethics of memory and, 154–55; faith after, 73; historical approach to, 3; as historical narrative, 89–90, 94; Israeli society and, 9–10; memoirs about, 87–90; Middle Eastern Jews and, 16; "Never forget," 22; pluralistic nature of truth recognized in, 19, 95–96; ritualizations of, 97–98; survivors, loss of, 14–15, 86–87, 88; theological responses to, 94–98; *yizker bikher*, 89–90, 97; Yom HaShoah, 4, 6–7

Holocaust denial, 93–94

Holocaust fatigue, 92–93

honor of God or *kavod*, 51, 53, 55–56

"Hope, Despair, and Memory" (Wiesel), 1

*hora'at sha'ah*, 84, 93

Hosea, book of, 72

"How Do We Understand the Holocaust?" (Franklin), 81

huppah or wedding canopy, Sinai associated with, 34, 71–72

hurban or cataclysm, 23–24, 81–98, 146; as brokenness, rupture, or caesura, 14, 84–85, 95–97; *hora'at sha'ah*, 84, 93; "radical continuity" of rabbis in face of, 36, 82, 85–86; ritualizations of, 85–86, 97–98; Second Temple, destruction of, 36, 81–86; theological responses to, 82–86, 94–98. *See also* Holocaust

Hushim, son of Dan, 40–41

identity, Jewish: *ahavah* and, 67; cognitive dissonance and, 19; distorted memory and, 136; in history versus mythic imagination, 2, 8, 10–11; hurban and, 86, 94, 95; modernity and, 146, 149, 154; in Pittsburgh Platform, 12; place of memory in, 25–27; *teshuva* and, 100, 103, 111; *yir'ah*, role of, 58–59

*Igerot HaReiyah* (Kook), 25

infants. *See* children

*In Search of Memory* (Kandel), 20

Isaiah, book of, 119

Israel: American Jewish community's

connection to, 148–49; history and memory in, 9–12, 15; Song of Songs as metaphor for founding of, 70–71; Yom HaZikaron, 4, 6

I-Thou relational theology, 66

Rabbi Jacob, 1–2

Jacob (biblical patriarch), 40–41

Jeremiah, book of, 119

Job, book of, 97, 118

Joseph (biblical patriarch), 40

Rabbi Joshua, 83–84, 93, 98, 113, 114

Judges, book of, 71, 94, 127

Judt, Tony, 15

Kabbalah, 6, 65, 66–67

*kabbalah* or receiving, 38, 112

Kafka, Franz, 57, 125, 137–39, 141

Kandel, Eric, 20–22

Katz, Jacob, 111

*kavod* or honor of God, 51, 53, 55–56

Kimchi, Rabbi David (RaDaK), 69–70

Kings, biblical books of, 71

*k'neged*, 150, 151

knowledge: commandedness and, 29–30; Eden story and, 27–28, 35–36, 54, 57, 74, 125, 150. *See also* enlightenment, parable of garden of

"Kol Dodi Dofek" or "The Voice of My Beloved Knocketh" (Joseph Soloveitchik), 70–71

*Kol Israel arevim zo b'zo*, 33–34

Kook, Rabbi Abraham Isaac, 25, 125–26

Lansky, Aaron, 92

Levenson, Jon, 34, 141

Leviticus, 28

Levitt, Laura, 102

Liebes, Yehuda, 65

Linsky, Marty, 151

Lipstadt, Deborah, 93–94

literary and artistic output regarding Holocaust, 87, 90, 93, 94

liturgical calendar, Jewish: "memory season" in, 4–7; *yir'ah* or awe in, 44–45. *See also specific holidays and holy days*

love. *See ahavah* or love

75; hiddenness, eroticism of, 74;
Hosea, accusations of whoredom
in, 72; problematic texts, mishnah
on study of, 53–56; prostitution, 72,
118, 126, 131; Rehume, parable of,
68, 69; Sinai, revelation at, 65–66,
72; in Song of Songs, 70–71

Shabbat Zakhor, 4–5

Shamor and Zakhor commandments,
30–31, 39

Shavuot, 4, 5, 6

Shema, 61, 63, 64, 75–76

Shoah. See Holocaust

shofar, 82

shtetl photographs of Roman Vishniac,
135–37

sight, belief, and understanding, 46–53,
55, 58–59, 120–23

Sinai, revelation at: Auschwitz and,
94–95; as betrothal between God
and people of Israel, 34, 71–72;
departure of children of Israel from,
144–45, 146; erotic associations
of, 65–66, 72; formative memory,
as place of, 34–35; masoret and
kabbalah, as process of, 38; midrash
combining commandment with
threat regarding, 62; presence of
converts at, 31, 33; Shamor and
Zakhor commandments, 30–31

Sinai and Zion (Levenson), 34

sixth sense, memory as, 147

Soloveitchik, Haim, 13–14, 23

Soloveitchik, Rabbi Joseph, 70–71, 139–40

Song of Songs, 70–71

sovereign self, concept of, 18–19, 110,
139–40

Spinoza (Strauss), 99

Spinoza, Baruch, 2

story and memory, relationship between,
104–6

Strauss, Leo, 99–100

Streicher, Julius, 5

sympathetic reading, importance of,
22–23, 76, 142

Talmud: Tractate Hagigah, 117–18 (see also
enlightenment, parable of garden

of); Tractate Ketubot, 67–69; Tractate Niddah, 29, 47; Tractate Shabbat,
30; Tractate Shavuot, 30; Tractate
Sotah, 40

tarbut ra'ah (polluted practice), 118

tefillin/phylacteries, 63, 66, 72

Temple, destruction of, 36, 81–86

teshuva (return, restoration, repentance),
24, 99–115, 146; authenticity and,
114–15; continuity, rhetoric of,
112–13; enlightenment, parable of
garden of, 132; history, cross-
cultural, 113–14; Jewish peoplehood
and diversity, 110–12; modernity,
Jewish experience of, 99–100, 111;
personal nature of memory and,
100–104; restoration of collective
memory and, 105–10; revitalization of concept of, 141; story and
memory, relationship between,
104–6; traditional views of, 107–9

therapy, mitzvah or commandedness in, 27

Tiele, Cornelius, 57

To Mend the World (Fackenheim), 107

Torah: Golden Rule as great principle of,
75, 143–44; importance of study
of, 149–52; reception of (see Sinai,
revelation at)

Torat Kohanim, 28

Tosefta Sotah, 83–84

tractates, Talmudic. See Talmud

transmission or masoret, 38, 112

tree metaphor in Christian and rabbinic
theology, 32–33

truth: accuracy versus, 137; pluralistic
nature of, 19–20, 95–96

Tucker, Rabbi Ethan, 22–23

tzitzit, 59

ultra-Orthodox Judaism, 109

understanding, belief, and sight, 46–53,
55, 58–59, 120–23

Understanding the Sick and the Healthy
(Rosenzweig), 106–7

U.S. Holocaust Memorial Museum, Washington, D.C., 87, 92–93

universalism and particularism: cognitive
dissonance, resolving, 18; continu-